the robert pattinson album

the robert pattinson album

paul stenning

plexus, london

contents

introduction

'I can't see any advantage to being famous,
because I'm happy with the life I have now.
I've got the same two friends I've had since I was
twelve, and I can't see that changing.'
– Robert Pattinson

Still in his early twenties, Robert Pattinson has already garnered lavish and gushing praise for his acting abilities, making the devastatingly handsome Londoner one of the hottest British sensations to hit the big screen in years.

His rise has been nothing short of meteoric, and mimics the way in which many young stars are catapulted into the limelight – instantly overexposed and with immense expectation placed upon a relatively limited body of work. 'So many young people who get a big hit kind of get hyped up,' Robert has said. 'They start to believe their own hype and then everyone starts to, like, cut them down immediately. And I just feel like I'm being propelled by something I have absolutely no control over.'

But Robert Pattinson is no temporary talent. His love of his art, which is of course the most important element of any successful and lengthy career, comes first and is a genuine passion, schooled by hours of Jack Nicholson movies and years of amateur theatrics. 'Robert has wanted to be an actor for as long as I can remember,' said his aunt, Monica Weller.

He rose from drama club and bit parts relatively quickly, but earnestly and intelligently, taking on roles that lesser, even older actors might have felt overwhelmed by. Barely out of his teens, Robert was re-enacting the life of Salvador Dali for the silver screen. Pattinson's captivatingly accurate performance in *Little Ashes* betrayed an ardent skill belying his years, and the intensive preparation with which he shaped the role was indicative of everything that makes him so very special.

Despite his appearance in two of the monstrously successful *Harry Potter* movies, Robert Pattinson's work to date reveals a greater fondness for low-budget experimentation than any Hollywood blockbuster. 'Expectations never really mean anything to me,' he said. 'I don't really care what people's expectations are of anything.' His role as Cedric Diggory in *Harry Potter And The Goblet Of Fire* was particularly

Crazy, sexy, cool: Robert at the October 2008 premiere
of teen gross-out movie Sex Drive *in Los Angeles.*

impressive, yet his ultimate accolade to date typifies the Londoner's brief yet dazzling career. It also proves that he has the Midas touch when it comes to breathing life into a modest production.

When Pattinson signed up for three *Twilight* movies, beating three thousand other aspiring Edward Cullen's, he was unaware of just how gargantuan his role would become. ('I went into it when it was a trilogy and signed on for the next two,' he revealed. 'But I guess it depends on how much money each of them makes.') Nor could he have foreseen the elaboration of a franchise which began with Stephenie Meyer's best-selling *Twilight* novels, and has since swelled exponentially thanks, in no small part, to his mesmerising portrayal of Edward. 'The thing is, he looks different when he does characters,' said Meyer. 'When you watch the films that he's done, you might not be able to put [them] together with the same person because he's such a chameleon. There were times where he was just being Rob

> 'I hope success hasn't really changed me at all. I mean, I don't feel like it has. I don't feel any different to what I did before. I guess my friends would have to judge me, but I don't feel any different.'
> – Robert Pattinson

and then you'd hear "Action!" and he'd step into character – and he'd look different! He'd sound like Edward! It was crazy. He did such a good job.' Not only has Pattinson brought Edward Cullen to life onscreen, he moreover displays an enormous range and adaptability which will no doubt stand him in good stead for the future.

He can apply his myriad talents to any role, whether light, dark, or anything in between. The remarkable malleability and chameleonic nature of his abilities will guarantee enviable access to A-list scripts and ensure him an enduring career – vital, potent and varied.

Yet Pattinson is not one to take up a part lightly, and as his star rises further he shall doubtless encounter a limitless choice of roles. So far he has chosen wisely, and this looks set to continue if he is to seek a fulfilling career rather than an occupation grudgingly defined by a one-hit wonder.

Within his own right, Robert is already a superstar – a spectacularly talented, unique young actor who has proven himself able to successfully assume a multitude of different personas. And it seems certain that, with time, his skills will only increase in depth, diversity and accomplishment.

Robert wore a red velvet jacket which he had bought in a charity shop, to the London premiere of Harry Potter And The Goblet Of Fire *(November 2005).*

early years

'My parents are always saying,
"Oh, we're so proud of you," and I'm always like,
"Why?" It's just luck – I haven't done anything.'
– Robert Pattinson

Robert Thomas Pattinson was born in a private clinic near Barnes on 13 May, 1986, a distinctly beautiful and cherubic child from the outset. His mother and father, later described in the press as 'arty', are Richard, who ran a successful business importing vintage cars from America, and Clare, who worked for a modelling agency. The couple met through a mutual family friend in a pub in Richmond, Surrey. Clare had grown-up with two older sisters in a humble household in close proximity to the prosperous Richmond Hill area. Richard was originally from Redcar, Yorkshire, a seaside resort in north-east England. They married when Clare was twenty-six and Richard thirty-five.

'My dad is from Yorkshire and he did a bunch of things,' said Robert. 'In the Seventies, he moved to America for a bit and just worked as a taxi driver. Then he started selling cars in the Eighties. My mum worked as a booker at a modelling agency, and now they're both retired.'

Robert was raised in Barnes, a suburb of the London Borough of Richmond upon Thames. The River Thames cascades alongside the quiet town, an area similar in affluence and stature to the popular districts of Fulham and Chelsea, though regarded as a much quieter alternative to those bustling hotspots.

Some properties in the Barnes vicinity fetch upwards of a million pounds, and Robert grew up in a five-bedroom, semi-detached Victorian house typical of the region. There were few monetary worries for the Pattinson children during their formative years, yet all three (Robert and his sisters Elizabeth and Victoria) were taught the value of money and expected to contribute to the household. They were encouraged to earn their own income, albeit only in small amounts here and there. Elizabeth worked weekends at a local library. Robert was occasionally paid for dog-walking by a friend of his mother's, and began a regular paper round as soon as he was old enough. 'I started doing a paper round when I was about ten,' he said. 'I started earning £10 a week and then I was obsessed with earning money until I was about fifteen.'

Isn't he lovely: Robert's classic good looks were the key to his early film success.

Equally, given his sensible parents, it is likely Robert did not *feel* rich. Partly due to his being one of three children and partly because he was raised correctly, Robert was neither spoiled nor made to fear hard work. On the contrary, his mother and father instilled a strong work ethic and sense of morality in their son as soon as they were able. Clare Pattinson, a firm believer in the benefits of a balanced diet, was always keen to extol the virtues of a good Savoy cabbage to her children.

Barnes may seem like a sleepy suburb, but it boasts numerous musical connections. Among them is the famous Olympic Studios, housed on Church Road. Countless household names have recorded there, the Beatles and Rolling Stones among them. In more recent times Massive Attack, Madonna and Coldplay have also occupied the studio.

The Bull's Head pub, which faces the River Thames, is situated at the end of Lonsdale Road. This venue is also legendary in the music world, being a renowned jazz hotspot, often cited as the 'suburban Ronnie Scott's'. Barnes is also infamous as the scene of T. Rex singer Marc Bolan's fatal car crash near Gipsy Lane in 1977, where there is now a shrine in his honour. Today Barnes is home to many high-profile broadcasters, politicians and actors. Despite his overwhelming fame,

> 'Up until I was twelve my sisters used to dress me up as a girl and introduce me as "Claudia".'
> – Robert Pattinson

Robert Pattinson still calls Barnes home, stating in various interviews: 'I *need* London.'

A short drive away from the river leads to East Sheen, the site of Robert's first school. Tower House Preparatory is an independent boys-only school for children aged four to thirteen. Though Robert's parents taught him exemplary basics before the age of four, his learning and development was augmented with a first-class education, buoying an early passion for music and drama. 'I have been playing the piano for my entire life – since I was three- or four-years-old,' he has said. Students at Tower House are taught both in groups and as individuals, and it was here that Robert received valuable one-on-one tuition.

As the school's secretary reveals, 'Tower House offers half-hour speech and drama lessons during the day. These comprise of individual or paired sessions with personal, intensive lessons which throughout the year encompass acting and performance skills, improvisation, speaking for an audience, and posture and voice coaching. They work towards using these skills in school productions, speaking in class or assembly and performance readings. Drama club is also available to juniors and seniors to help the children with their acting skills, where they will gain invaluable experience in performing in front of people in a relaxed, uninhibited environment.'

By the age of six Robert was performing in amateur productions. One of his teachers wrote a play entitled *Spell For A Rhyme*, in which Robert won his first role, that of the mystical King of Hearts. Of course, like many young boys that age, Robert was less interested in serious acting and far more enthusiastic about playing with toys, not to mention his sisters. He was a slight and coy child, permeated by a natural, endearing timidity, both sociable and shy. Robert had inherited his father's laidback disposition and his mother's striking good looks. With both his sisters outranking their sibling, the youngest Pattinson was at their mercy when it came to playing games. He recalled, 'Up until I was twelve my sisters used to dress me up as a girl and introduce me as "Claudia".'

It was difficult to misbehave at Tower House given its strict regimen and intolerance of typical bad boys' antics. Robert was not an unruly child by any means, but he stood out as being particularly untidy. In a 1998 school newsletter he was described as the 'runaway winner of last term's Form Three untidy desk award'. This was about as far as his indiscretions ran – most rebellious was his blatant refusal to do homework. This was not because he couldn't follow the syllabus or due to errant laziness, rather it just didn't seem important to him. 'I really wasn't very much of a rebel,' he admitted. 'I'm seen by people now as more of a rebel, which is strange. I don't like doing what people tell me to do. [But] I don't deliberately rebel against them.' It was nonchalance, not resistance, which formed the basis of

School days: A photograph of Rob taken during his time at Tower House School. According to their 1998 school newsletter Robert was the runaway winner of the 'untidy desk award'.

Pattinson's lackadaisical attitude. As he has since revealed, 'School reports were always pretty bad – I never ever did my homework. I always turned up for lessons as I liked my teachers, but my report said I didn't try very hard.'

'I started doing a newspaper round when I was about ten.' – Robert Pattinson

Robert's school reports led his parents to harbour some doubts about their son's direction. He would spend more time staring out of the window than doing actual academic work. 'I like looking out the window,' Robert admitted. 'I'm pretty relaxed most of the time.'

Other than being dressed as a girl by his sisters, Robert's childhood leisure pursuits were unremarkable. He regularly played football, and enjoyed watching cartoons, as he has since confirmed. 'I quite liked *Sharky And George*, and then there was a cartoon with rapper MC Hammer in it – *Hammertime* – I loved that cartoon, it was genius! They don't make cartoons like that anymore.' (*Sharky And George* was an animation about two detective fish who solved crimes underwater. Robert may also have confused the MC Hammer cartoon with one of Hammer's popular catchphrases. The show Robert enjoyed was actually called *Hammerman* and featured MC Hammer as a hero who wore magical dancing shoes.)

Robert also took a musical lead from MC Hammer, deciding he wanted to front a rap posse. 'When I was fourteen, I fronted a rap trio,' he said, admitting to being a teenage admirer of artists including Eminem and Jamiroquai, claiming that his band was 'pretty hardcore for three private school kids from suburban London. And my mum's, like, cramping our style, popping her head in to ask, "You boys want a sandwich?"'

However, early on in life Robert developed a knack for drama, and it was this which saved him from early recriminations over his other imprudence. After his part in *Spell For A Rhyme*, Robert appeared in the school's adaptation of William Golding's *Lord Of The Flies*, synonymously playing the role of Robert.

Although he found plenty of time to devote to more basic hobbies ('I sort of consider myself a geek. I went to a few [sci-fi conventions] in England, like *Doctor Who* ones, and I always found them really interesting. I guess I was a geek. But I was more of a computer-game geek; I wasn't really a comic-book geek'), Robert was encouraged to develop a sense of self and follow his own path, and clearly felt free to express himself in any way he wished without fear of being judged. The rather selective schooling he underwent certainly

> **'My school reports were always pretty bad – I never ever did my homework. I always turned up for lessons as I liked my teachers, but my report said I didn't try very hard.'**
> **– Robert Pattinson**

aided his development. Robert was fortunate enough to receive close tutoring and the encouragement necessary for him to fulfil his creative potential.

With many children a lack of academic achievement often reaps criticism from both parents and teachers – a prompt to improve grades 'or else'. With Robert, however, neither his parents nor the school staff were concerned with his lack of basic scholastic skills, simply because they knew he had talent and inspiration in other areas. As Caroline Booth, school secretary at Tower House, told the *London Evening Standard*, 'Robert wasn't a particularly academic child but he always loved drama. He was an absolutely lovely boy, everyone adored him. We have lots of lovely boys here but he was something special. He was very pretty, beautiful and blonde.' With his dark blue eyes and thatch of blonde hair (which would later darken), Robert naturally fulfilled the criterion of classic beauty.

Indeed, Robert developed his now familiar charm at an early age, which excused him from any major criticism. When he was guilty of the odd indiscretion it was generally assumed that he meant no real harm. It would appear that Robert stood out, for looks, charisma and his innate theatrical talents, but according to the school secretary he was not instantly recognisable as a future acting star. Caroline Booth said, 'I wouldn't say he was a star but he was very keen on our drama club, I do remember that.' She added of Robert's eventual fame: 'We're all so pleased that he's found something he really shines at.'

While Robert was still just a young boy he had already acquired his first admirers. Very soon, however, they would remember him for far more than simply being an adorable child. Within just a few years he would be lauded as one of the world's most talked-about young actors, making an unforgettable mark far beyond the sleepy hub of Barnes.

At the November 2005 Tokyo press conference for
Harry Potter And The Goblet Of Fire.

natural talent

'I wasn't at all focused at school,
and I didn't achieve much. But I've got a sense of urgency
now. I feel I can't let any more time waste away.'
– Robert Pattinson

When Robert turned twelve he left Tower House to attend the independent Harrodian School in Barnes, which, being situated on Lonsdale Road, was closer to the Pattinson family home. This came at a cost of £4,000 per term – a price which guaranteed Robert expert tutelage and endless opportunities for inspiration.

Robert has stated that he was expelled at the age of twelve ('I got expelled from my school when I was twelve. I was quite bad!'), though there seems to be a strong possibility that this was a throwaway remark, and one which he later refused to discuss.

The Harrodian School was opened by the present Chairman, Sir Alford Houstoun-Boswall, and his then-wife, Lady Eliana Houstoun-Boswall. The couple had to pay £5 million for the grounds, which were previously the property of Harrods owner Mohammed Al-Fayed, hence the name Harrodian.

The school housed only sixty-five pupils and twelve staff when it was founded in 1993, five years before Robert began attending. Upon his arrival, the rapidly growing but still coy Pattinson found himself amongst girls for the first time after eight years in an all-boys environment. ('I was twelve when I had my first kiss,' he later confessed.) He was also surrounded by pupils from a wide variety of age groups – everyone from four- to eighteen-year-olds. 'Twelve was a turning point, as I moved to a mixed school,' he said, adding, with tongue planted firmly in-cheek, 'and then I became cool and discovered hair gel.'

Sir Alford Houstoun-Boswall was adamant that his school should be the pinnacle of perfection and a unique platform for young minds. He believed it his duty to not only teach pupils the broadest and most useful knowledge available, but also to school them in manners and consideration for others. In particular, children were taught to be articulate in English and confident in French. 'I speak French, sort of,' Robert said. 'At, like, a three-year-old's standard.'

The school itself was luxurious, set over some twenty-five sprawling acres which were

In March 2006 Robert was a guest on kids' television show,
Holly and Stephen's Saturday Showdown.

geared towards athletics and field sports. Principal to Robert's development was the inclusion of drama studies in his curriculum. This was no footnote within his wider studies; it was a serious and encouraged pastime. There was also emphasis on art and music, but it was acting that Robert devoted himself to as he entered his teens.

He was a valued student once again, and was even given the responsibility of becoming a lunch monitor. 'I used to take everyone's chips!' he quipped. Occasionally he would break the defining habit of his school career and actually complete his homework. He excelled at English, his favourite lesson, and this was in part inspired by his favourite teacher, who seemingly couldn't find the wherewithal to criticise him in any way. 'She got me into writing instead of just answering the question,' Robert said. 'I used to hand in homework with twenty pages of nonsense and she'd still mark it. She was a really amazing teacher.'

Robert briefly flirted with the idea of becoming involved in politics, despite subsequently admitting that he was anything but focused in the classroom. 'I didn't achieve much,' he stated, 'but politics was what I wanted to do while I was in school, yeah. I just liked the whole idea of it. I wanted to be involved with politics. That's what my whole plan was. I was going to go to university and then I just thought, "Ah, I can't be bothered to do anything. I don't want to do any more homework!"' It was becoming clear that a career in the arts might be more appropriate for the free-spirited Pattinson.

> 'My dad spotted a bunch of girls in a café and they were all really excited, so he asked them where they'd been. When they said they'd been to drama classes, he reckoned I should get myself down there.'
> – Robert Pattinson

Though Harrodian itself produced high-quality drama productions, Robert was persuaded to enrol in the local Barnes Theatre Company as his acting abilities continued to develop. ('I really wasn't part of the acting fraternity at my school,' he explained.) Here he would star in his first major roles in plays such as *Anything Goes*, *Our Town* and *Tess Of The D'Urbervilles*.

'I started doing plays when I was about fifteen or sixteen,' Robert said. 'I only did it because my dad saw a bunch of pretty girls in a restaurant and he asked them where they came from and they said drama group. He said, "Son, that is where you need to go."' After the girls had mentioned Barnes Theatre Company, Robert's dad 'nagged me about attending. At one point he said he would pay me, which is pretty strange – I don't know what his intentions were, but I went.'

It was a light-hearted jape – a 'social thing', in Robert's words – yet this suggestion from his father was rooted in earnest parental wishes. Richard Pattinson had hoped that his youngest child would pursue acting, partly because he wanted his children involved in the arts, but mostly because he genuinely believed his son possessed extraordinary talent and ability. Robert also feels that his father may have harboured creative aspirations which he sought to realise through his children. 'My dad said to me, "I really am an artistic person." I was shocked as I never saw him as creative. I think me and my sisters are living out that side of him.'

The acting bug had indeed already taken root in the Pattinson family. It was initially expected that Robert's sister Elizabeth (Lizzy for short), who was three years his senior, would go into the profession. The beautiful, five-foot-eight, green-eyed blonde embarked on an early performing career, appearing in creditable plays such as Paddy Gormley's *Misanthrope II* and Ian Buckley's *The Return*. Lizzy explored numerous styles and even tried her hand at comedic sketches. Yet it was with dance and music that she felt most comfortable. She had been awarded a Grade Eight in ballet before deciding that, with her alto voice, she was talented enough to make it in the music business. In fact, her vocals were so note-perfect that she contributed to several session recordings.

Lizzy took to performing at various small clubs and pubs in the Barnes vicinity – including the Sun Inn – and in Central London. It was on one of these bigger performance nights that, whilst only seventeen, Lizzy was spotted by a talent scout working for the EMI record label. He decided to invite the talented singer to become a member of the dance band Aurora. The band released two tracks which graced the UK Top 20 – 'Dreaming' and 'The Day It Rained Forever'. Unusually for a dance troupe, they toured, being more than capable of reproducing their material live. Shows took place in the UK as well as Europe and North America, and on one occasion they performed to over 100,000 people. After collaborating with Milk & Sugar, the house music producers and DJs, Lizzy secured a Number One *Billboard* Dance Chart hit in the US with 'Let The Sunshine In', which also charted at Number 16 in the UK. (Lizzy's name would also eventually appear on the *Twilight* credits; she added background vocals to the soundtrack of several scenes that Robert appeared in.)

> 'I auditioned for *Guys And Dolls* and got a little tiny part as some Cuban dancer or something, and then in the next play I got the lead part, and then I got my agent.'
> – Robert Pattinson

She is now pursuing a solo music career but, according to her online résumé, remains available for acting duties as and when required. Victoria Pattinson, who is two years older than her sister, has so far been the only Pattinson child to pursue a more regular line of work, plying her trade at an advertising agency.

There was never a specific career goal in Robert Pattinson's mind, given his characteristically carefree attitude. 'I never really had any aspirations to be an actor when I was young,' he said. 'I wanted to play the piano in a bar, be the old dude with a whisky glass, all dishevelled.' There was no master plan for world domination or a burning desire to win an Oscar, and he would have been quite comfortable following in the footsteps of either Lizzy or Victoria. Indeed, he has suggested that had he not turned to acting professionally he would have 'just gone to university and would have kind of just done the average thing'.

Even when he became part of the Barnes Theatre Company, Robert was less than specific about his future desires, often working in the wings on technical aspects of the plays rather than acting. Still, within the bounds of the club, Robert was in a perfect place to realise his potential. And his dad was not about to let him hide behind the stage – he knew his son was destined for greater things. Indeed, Robert would later speculate that his father had 'some sort of weird foresight' regarding his son's career path, owing to the fact that the two of them had argued for a long time over whether he should join the company.

The Barnes Theatre Company had a good pedigree, so it was a convenient choice in terms of location and reputation. Robert appeared as one of the dancers in a production of *Guys And Dolls* before securing a full acting part in the next play, *A Little Night Music*. After this, he was discovered by an agent through his performance in *Tess Of The D'Urbervilles*.

'So many people from there had become actors,' Robert said. 'Rusty and Ann, who are the directors, were actors themselves and were very talented. They were a very good group, and for some reason when I finished the backstage thing, I just decided that I should try to act. So I auditioned for *Guys And Dolls* and got a little tiny part as some Cuban dancer or something, and then in the next play I got the lead part, and then I got my agent.'

It was during this period that Robert met his long-term friend Tom Sturridge, who was just five months older than Pattinson, and the son of Charles Sturridge, a director well-known for his work on *Brideshead Revisited*, *Shackleton*, and numerous other films and TV adaptations. Early on, Robert and Tom found themselves locked in a friendly rivalry, often auditioning for the same parts. 'We go up against each other every single time,' said Robert, 'even though we look completely different.' In fact, Robert's very first film, *Vanity Fair*, also featured a small part for Tom Sturridge, though they have not appeared together in anything since.

> **'I was modelling at twelve, the youngest person in my agency out of the girls or boys. I was so ridiculously skinny…'**
> **– Robert Pattinson**

Of the Barnes Theatre Company, Robert has stated the he 'owes everything to that little club', given that his appearances on stage brought him to wider attention, and very quickly so. Acting was still more of a hobby rather than a potential vocation but, with careful sway from his parents, in particular his father, he was beginning to realise he could make a career out of this burgeoning talent. From here on in, Robert Pattinson's life would progress at a vastly accelerated pace.

Robert's brief but accomplished work for the Barnes Theatre Company led his agent to scout for television roles – the first port of call for up-and-coming actors and actresses fresh out of the theatre. In the meantime, however, Robert performed to his biggest audience yet in William Shakespeare's *Macbeth* at the Old Sorting Office, a charitable trust which houses the OSO Arts Centre. This venue, which is based on Barnes Common, opened in 2002 and features a range of performing arts projects, from plays to art exhibitions and musical performances.

Though the OSO was predominantly intended for local budding artists to try their

Model behaviour: Photos from Robert's early career as a teen model.

hand at anything and everything performance-related, they were also lucky enough to feature the occasional professional play, such as *Macbeth*. This was a place for amateurs to receive advice and improve their craft.

By now, however, Robert Pattinson was more in need of contacts in television and movies than any acting coaching. In fact, aside from his stints in various schools and clubs, he had received next to no formal training. It was nothing more than a natural ability that had seen him develop with limited professional advice or guidance. Fatefully, Robert nurtured this gift and began to thrive, despite the fact that for a long time he was unsure of his precise career plans.

At a young age, Robert had also been coerced into modelling as a result of his mother's association with a leading European agency for male and female models. He worked for fashion designer Nicole Farhi and the Hackett clothing line, as well as doing regular shoots for spreads in teen magazines. 'I was doing it at twelve,' Robert has since explained, 'the youngest person in my agency out of the girls or boys. I was so ridiculously skinny I looked like a girl, but that was the period where they loved androgynous-looking people.'

He had the looks and the charm to be a top model, as one glance at his professional résumé attests. We can learn that he wears a size 10.5 shoe (UK size, in the US this is an 11) and has a remarkably narrow waist – just 25.5 inches. He takes a fourteen-inch collar, has a thirty-six-inch chest, and is six-foot two-inches tall.

'I always get referred to as an ex-model,' he complained, 'and, like, I maybe did three jobs. I did like women's ring modelling. I used to do it in catalogues 'cause I have very feminine hands. Still do.'

The seed of inspiration for Robert's forays into more professional climes had been

Barnes boy: Four photos of Robert performing with Barnes Theatre Company, the amateur dramatics group he later credited with being responsible for his success.

sown when Pattinson was just thirteen, and happened to see the epic drama *One Flew Over The Cuckoo's Nest*. This 1975 adaptation of the classic novel by Ken Kesey starred Jack Nicholson as R. P. McMurphy, a patient who rebels against the tyrannical rules of a mental asylum. (Randle Patrick McMurphy was also allegedly an alias used by Robert on the social networking site Facebook.)

From that moment on, Robert Pattinson decided that Nicholson was his hero and copied everything about him. 'I used to be so timid,' he said, 'and that was one of those films that [helped me break out] by pretending to be Randle.' He read all he could on the lauded actor and watched many of his other movies. 'I think he is literally the only actor who I can guarantee if I see a Jack Nicholson movie which I haven't seen, even though I've seen them all now… It's like a seal of approval. So, you know that there's something going to be worth watching about the movie. Every single thing he's done. It's bizarre.' He also began to mimic Nicholson, whose familiar character traits seem to permeate each one of his performances. 'I aspire to be Jack Nicholson,' Pattinson confessed. 'I love his every single mannerism. I used to try and be him in virtually everything I did, I don't know why. After I watched *One Flew Over The Cuckoo's Nest* I dressed like him. I tried to do his accent. I did everything like him. I think it kind of stuck with me.'

Pattinson was clearly aiming high, given that Jack Nicholson is one of the most respected and admired actors of the last fifty years, having won accolades and awards many times over. Another one of his favourite film icons was Jean-Luc Godard, and he often espoused the French director's style and body of work. '*Prenom Carmen*, which sounds like I'm just saying that to be cool, but it's actually one of my favourite films,' Robert said of one of Godard's strongest works. 'I think it's the best Godard film. It's like his version of *Carmen* the opera, one of his films from the Eighties. In terms of just pure filmmaking and manipulating an audience, it kind of starts out as a farce, as a complete, stupid farce, with this bank robbery; but it's really, really Godardian, with kind of a stupid humour that's so random. Only he could make it, mixed up with these kinds of philosophical elements.'

Robert Pattinson's first film role was in the costume drama *Vanity Fair*, which starred Gabriel Byrne and Reese Witherspoon. He was to be disappointed, however, when the scenes he had filmed were cut out of the final product. Thankfully these were not lost and appear in the 'extras' of the film's DVD. Ever modest, Robert said of the experience: 'My first job I was playing Reese Witherspoon's son and I hadn't done any acting in school. I wasn't in a drama school or anything. I'd done one amateur play and you end up doing a film with Reese Witherspoon.'

> 'I wouldn't be acting if it wasn't for Barnes Theatre Club…
> I owe everything to that little club. In a weird sort of way, that stuff was probably the best I've done and the stuff I am most proud of.'
> – Robert Pattinson

Adapted from the famous novel by William Makepeace Thackeray, *Vanity Fair* was directed by Mira Nair and released in 2004. There have been, and surely will continue to be, many TV and film versions of the story – which follows the trials and tribulations of Becky Sharp (Witherspoon), as she escapes an impoverished childhood and establishes herself within the upper regions of 19th-century British aristocracy – but Nair's version seemed to garner apathy rather than abject distaste or praise. It was perhaps most notable for an ending that altered the original plot; a conclusion happier than that found in the novel.

Though Witherspoon is in reality only ten years older than Robert, she played his mother in the film. Perhaps this is one reason why his scenes were deleted from the movie, considering Witherspoon was not exactly made to look much older than her twenty-seven years. As Robert himself said, 'She was twenty-seven at the time and it was ridiculous!'

Witherspoon, however, remembered it as a pleasant experience. Asked four years later what she recalled of working with the now famous Robert Pattinson, she swooned, 'I remember he was verrrrry handsome! I was like, "I have a really handsome son!" I had to sob and cry all over him, but he was great.'

Left: *Another day, another photo shoot with a teen magazine.* Right: *A hairdressing magazine makes use of Robert's edgy good looks to show off the latest trends.*

Robert was uncredited in the film, though he was still paid – his very first paid acting job. Despite the absence of his scenes in the finished movie, the prestige of sharing the bill with such praised actors proved one thing for certain: Robert Pattinson belonged in this company and could excel when given the chance. It also gave casting directors in Hollywood word of this bright young talent who had a terrific amount of potential and was still only in his late teens. 'When I was seventeen,' he later reflected, 'I was so much cooler because I knew less about myself.'

During his time on the set he was treated just like any other actor. As he explained, 'You have a trailer and stuff. It was the most ridiculous thing. And I was thinking, "I should be an actor. I'm doing a movie with Reese Witherspoon. How is this happening?" It's the one job where you can do whatever you want and people have got to accept it. If you were going to an office, got upset and said, "I need to go punch out some windows because I have to do this database," you'd get fired! But you get a lot of slack as an actor. You can just go nuts all the time.'

Just a few months after *Vanity Fair* Robert landed a part where his scenes would be included; indeed, he had a reasonably prominent role in the movie. Again he was performing alongside well-known actors, including Max Von Sydow (renowned for his collaborations with director Ingmar Bergman and his performance in 1973's *The Exorcist*, one of Robert's favourite films) and Julian Sands (whom Robert was to reunite with when filming *The Haunted Airman*). He was in esteemed company, also sharing the screen with Alicia Witt, who had appeared in the likes of *The Sopranos* and *Ally McBeal*. It was a varied and talented cast. 'I went to do my first big movie when I was seventeen,' Robert said of the shoot. 'I was in South Africa for three and a half months, and I was by myself.'

Confusingly the film, *Ring Of The Nibelungs*, is known by many different titles, including *Dark Kingdom: The Dragon King*, *Die Nibelungen*, *Curse Of The Ring*, and *Sword Of Xanten*. This is partly due to its destination country, Germany, though the film also found an outlet in Australia, the UK and USA. Dubbed into German, the TV movie hit

These pictures from Robert's portfolio emphasise the androgynous good looks that made him a successful model in his early teens.

screens on 29 November, 2004. It was Robert Pattinson's first fully credited screen appearance. *Die Nibelungen*, as it was known in Germany, became the highest rated mini-series on television that year. A year later it was also shown on the UK's Channel Four. They dubbed it a 'megafeature' and the title was then *Sword Of Xanten*.

Again Pattinson's was a supporting role, but thankfully this time his scenes were not deleted. The story revolves around Siegfried (played by German actor Benno Furmann), a young blacksmith who has a mighty alter ego and slays a dragon, thereby winning the heart of the warrior queen Brunhild (played by Kristanna Loken, previously seen as Arnold Schwarzenegger's nemesis in *Terminator 3*). As a reward for slaying the dragon, Siegfried receives a vast hoard of treasure – a prize that is wracked by a curse and threatens his future with the gorgeous queen. The story is based on Germanic and Nordic myths – the same legends which eventually inspired J.R.R. Tolkien to pen *The Lord Of The Rings* trilogy.

> **'When I first started I was quite tall and looked like a girl, so I got lots of jobs, because it was during that period where the androgynous look was cool.'**
> **– Robert Pattinson**

Pattinson plays Giselher, the young brother of King Gunther and Princess Kriemhild. Giselher idolises the blacksmith Siegfried as some sort of demigod. Intriguingly, no reviewers seemed to pick up on the dashing young Pattinson, who played his (limited) part superbly. Even BBC critic Jamie Russell was unmoved by the plethora of English talent starring in the movie, and – perhaps predictably – panned the film. His review termed *Ring Of The Nibelungs*, 'A Teutonic Tolkien cash-in light on brains, brawn and budget, *Xanten* is fantasy cinema at its least fantastic. Old warriors go to Valhalla, old actors go to German TV.'

There was no mention of potential star Robert Pattinson, the reviewers seemingly oblivious to his palpable charms. The *New York Times* were more lenient towards the

Left: *Robert in a deleted scene from* Vanity Fair, *in which he played the son of Reese Witherspoon's character, the conniving social climber Becky Sharp.* Right: *As Giselher in the German made-for-TV movie* Ring Of The Nibelungs.

movie, stating it was, 'Made for about $25 million but looks as if it cost much more, with lots of Nordic-seeming ice and mist, and a dragon that, for once, really looks like a dragon, squatty and lizard-like.'

Robert had kept up with a strict homework regime whilst filming in South Africa, although he missed a university interview due to his filming commitments. He used his earnings from modelling, *Vanity Fair* and *Ring Of The Nibelungs* to help fund his final years at the Harrodian School, after his father had expressed doubts about paying the fees required for him to complete his A-levels. 'At the time, my father said to me, "Okay, you might as well leave school now, since you're not working very hard." And when I told him I wanted to stay on for my A-levels, he said I'd have to pay my own fees – then he'd pay me back if I got good enough grades.' In the end, Robert achieved an A and two Bs at A-level, though his father's promised refund failed to materialise. 'I don't know how that happened. I didn't even know half the syllabus. I lost faith in the exam system at that point.'

> 'I never set out to be an actor, though I'd be quite annoyed if it fell apart, because I quite enjoy doing it.'
> – Robert Pattinson

Though it is unclear whether Pattinson's appearance in the film was seen by many casting agents or directors, Robert's accomplished performance in his first TV role certainly did him no harm. Just before flying to the exotic reaches of South Africa to film *Ring Of The Nibelungs*, he had been introduced to *Harry Potter And The Goblet Of Fire* director Mike Newell by a casting director. Following his return to London after filming was completed, and a subsequent secondary audition, Robert learned that he had received his first big break. After just one film appearance in which he didn't ultimately appear, and a solid if unspectacular fantasy title made for television, Robert had suddenly been accepted for the part of Cedric Diggory in the *Harry Potter* epic. Mike Newell would later state of Robert and his character: 'Cedric exemplifies all that you would expect the Hogwarts champion to be. Robert Pattinson was born to play the role; he's quintessentially English with chiselled public schoolboy good looks.'

From here on in, the sky would be the limit.

Robert arrives at the London premiere of House Of Wax *in May 2005*

hotter than potter

'Oh, Jesus! I used to get told I looked like Prince William from *Harry Potter!* Ah, it's terrible! It's the worst thing you could possibly have said… I'm trying to get away from that whole stigma of the floppy English posh person.'
— Robert Pattinson

Within a year of leaving school, eighteen-year-old Robert Pattinson had already shared camera time with Reese Witherspoon, travelled to South Africa, become a German TV star, and been picked to play a prominent role in the *Harry Potter* saga. *Harry Potter* meant that small and intimate was out of the question. The cast was massive, the sets were enormous and the budget was a jaw-dropping £76 million. Pattinson must have shuddered when he saw his name high up on the cast list, and alongside such veteran legends of the silver screen.

Names like Gary Oldman, Ralph Fiennes, Alan Rickman and Timothy Spall are synonymous with the lofty reaches of modern British cinema. And although Daniel Radcliffe was three years younger than Robert Pattinson, he was already universally acknowledged as a well-established actor, and as such deserving of a great deal of respect. 'At first I felt a bit of pressure,' Pattinson told one interviewer, 'but after a week, when all the cast were known, and they are all so nice, then the feeling was gone. When I was shooting my first scene, the maze scene, there was a crew of about one hundred and fifty people, me, Dan and the producer. Later on, it became about two thousand people involved in shooting. I'm really glad I could get started in a more relaxed environment and get used to it progressively.'

The cast members who really left young Robert star-struck were not those you might imagine. *Harry Potter And The Goblet Of Fire* also featured Michael Gambon and Warwick Davis, and it was the addition of these two actors in particular which most intrigued Pattinson. Gambon is a veteran Irish actor who has appeared in the likes of *Gosford Park* and *Sleepy Hollow*. At three-feet-six-inches tall, Warwick Davis's diminutive stature belies a larger-than-life persona, and arguably his biggest role came when he played Willow Ufgood in the 1988 swords-and-sorcery movie *Willow*. When Robert Pattinson was growing up he used to watch *Willow* regularly, to the point where it

Robert as Cedric Diggory in Harry Potter And The Goblet Of Fire, *the role that kick-started his Hollywood career.*

School reunion: the young cast of Harry Potter And The Goblet Of Fire *join director Mike Newell and producer David Heyman for a London photo shoot to publicise the film in October 2005.*

'On *Harry Potter* I was so conscious of the fact that I didn't know what I was doing, I used to sit on the side of the set throwing up.' – Robert Pattinson

became (and remains) one of his favourite films. He was therefore duly impressed when he found himself in a scene with his fellow Englishman. Robert laughed, 'I had one scene sitting next to him at the dragon task, and I had no idea what to say to him at all! He was the only person I asked for an autograph the whole way through it.'

Though the actor was not one of Robert's particular favourites, he nevertheless felt intimidated by the multi-talented Ralph Fiennes – as much by his reserved aura as his back catalogue. Indeed, Fiennes's résumé is tremendously impressive; he has appeared in almost forty movies, most notably *Schindler's List* and *The English Patient.*

'I didn't really talk to Ralph Fiennes while I was doing *Harry Potter* and the only thing I did with him was when he stepped on my head,' Pattinson recalled. 'Then I went to this play and he was there. And this girl said, "You've worked with Ralph Fiennes haven't you, Robert?" And I was like, "Well, no…" and Ralph said, "Yes, I stepped on your head." And that was the extent of our conversation.'

There was also the somewhat bizarre matter of performing alongside three iconic actors who were still little more than children. As well as Daniel Radcliffe, Robert worked with Rupert Grint and Emma Watson, who played Ron Weasley and Hermione Granger in all of the *Harry Potter* films.

Robert shows that he had already begun to develop his personal style and unique approach to grooming by the time he played Cedric.

'I did get star-struck a little bit by the three main young guys when I first met them, it was kind of strange,' Robert confessed. 'We did this rehearsal week and it was kind of weird meeting these three rather iconic kids, and just talking to them normally. I couldn't really get it out of my head, like "You're Harry Potter," but that was strange, but not really, everyone was very friendly. It's a very relaxed set.'

After a few days of bonding with Grint and Watson in particular, Robert was full of admiration for his new co-stars, both as grounded young people and impressive actors with plenty of natural ability.

Pattinson's character, Cedric Diggory, is a sixth-year Hufflepuff student at Hogwarts School of Witchcraft and Wizardry. He is also one of the Triwizard champions. In the book Diggory is identified as a 'good student who values fair play and honesty'.

Harry Potter And The Goblet Of Fire was the fourth part of the *Harry Potter* series, and as usual it featured Harry Potter (Radcliffe) doing battle with all manner of beastly foes, this time during the Triwizard Tournament. Cedric was essentially an archetypal good guy, but with a slight edge which Robert rather enjoyed. 'I think Cedric's a pretty cool character,' he explained. 'He's not really a complete cliché of the good kid in school. He's just quiet. He is actually just a genuinely good person, but he doesn't make a big deal about it or anything. He's just like, "Whatever." I can kind of relate to that. He's not an unattractive character at all and his storyline is a nice storyline to play.'

Not only did he have an attractive personality, Cedric was naturally a bit of a dish, too.

Top, from left to right: *French and English press features from the* Harry Potter *period.*
Bottom: *An autographed photo of Rob as Cedric hints at how his later nickname RPattz may have come about.*

In the original book, as well as the first script Robert was handed, Cedric Diggory is described as 'an absurdly handsome seventeen-year-old'. Never one to avoid humility, Robert was fairly uncomfortable with the prospect of having to live up to such a billing. It made him feel more concerned with how he looked on camera as opposed to remembering his lines or keeping in character.

'It kind of puts you off a little bit,' Robert quipped, 'when you're trying to act, and you're trying to get good angles to look good-looking and stuff. It's really stupid; you'd think I'm really egotistical. But I think that's the most daunting part about it – it's much scarier than meeting Voldemort [Ralph Fiennes's character]!'

At the start of filming it was decreed that Cedric should be ultra-fit and look as dashing as can be, and that Robert should also be able to cope with the physical demands of filming. 'I hadn't done anything for about six months before so I was a little bit unfit,' Robert admitted. 'I remember the costume designer saying when I was trying on swimming trunks, "Aren't you supposed to be fit? You could be playing a sissy poet or something." The next day I got a call from the assistant director about a personal training programme.'

Being paired with a personal trainer was an odd experience for Robert – though he

Top left: Robert pictured with his co-stars Emma Watson and Katie Leung at the film's Tokyo premiere in November 2005. Top right: Robert pictured at the London premiere with Rupert Grint and Clemence Poesy, November 2005. Below: A British newspaper article from November 2005 foretells Rob's future success.

relished the seriousness of having to train so hard for his part. The production team were equally committed. They assigned a member of the stunt team to train Robert towards peak fitness, which did not prove to be a simple task by any means. 'The stunt team are the most absurdly fit guys in the world,' Robert said. 'I can't even do ten press-ups. I did about three weeks of that, and in the end I think he got so bored of trying to force me to do it that he wrote it all down so that I could do it at home.' Whilst training at home Robert ended up hurting his shoulder, bringing his strict regimen to an abrupt end. The team had no choice but to accept Cedric Diggory just as he was.

Among the most memorable scenes in the film was the inclusion of the maze as described in the book. This was one of the most expensive sections of the movie and equally one of the hardest to film. Robert was thrown in at the deep end (literally, as it happened) and had to adjust to all of his new cast-mates as well as a tricky action sequence.

He described the experience of filming the maze as 'pretty intense. It was really difficult to translate all the things in the book that happened in the maze, like all these riddles and things, into film. It was almost impossible. The way Mike Newell did it was really good. He came up with the idea that in the maze it is just the fear and the darkness and the isolation that kind of drives all the competitors a bit insane. We were really hyped up. You are on one-hundred percent adrenaline.'

The maze scene's fierce camera angles clouded the audience with a sense of claustrophobia, something which the actors embraced rather than feared, especially Robert. 'In the maze, a lot of it was on steady cam – which is just a guy running around with a camera – and all the hedges moved,' he explained breathlessly. 'So me and Dan were basically chasing each other around and punching each other, with these hedges squeezing us. It was so real. And because it was all hydraulic walls, no one actually knew if it would kill you or not, if you actually got trapped there. So, it was quite nice to be doing enforced method acting.'

> 'The cemetery scene was the bit I was most looking forward to doing... No one has died in it so it's always going to be the first death in *Harry Potter*. It was cool, one of the best parts of the part I think.'
> – Robert Pattinson

Pattinson was used to the world of special effects, even from his brief career as it then stood. *Ring Of The Nibelungs* had featured a litany of effects, yet the budget was far smaller than that of *Harry Potter*, quite understandably. Robert felt comfortable adjusting to the epic nature of the *Potter* set, as it wasn't too far removed from his previous screen role; it merely had greater financial backing. In a relatively confined set space, two thousand people is a lot to contend with, but Robert took it in his stride, performing his lines with aplomb and making friends everywhere he went. Among these were two actors closer to Robert's age, who he felt he had even more in common with.

Katie Leung (who played Cho Chang), a young actress from Motherwell in Scotland, was appearing in her first feature film. So instantly there was a bond between the 'new guys' on set. 'I get on really well with Katie,' Robert said, 'she's a really cool girl. I don't have many talking scenes with her. Most of my scenes, like big scenes, are just with Dan. I dance with her, and there's a lot of scenes like holding hands and stuff like that. But I get on really well with her. She's a nice girl.'

Alongside Katie there was also Stanislav Ianevski (Viktor Krum in the film), a Bulgarian native who was exploring the movie-making world for the first time. Both Stanislav and Robert started on the same day, and bonded well as their respective parts often required them to film together on set.

For part of the movie Robert was required to go scuba diving and needed a crash course in the sport, all still within his first week on set. 'I had never done scuba diving before,' he recalled. 'I was in a tiny little tub that was a practice tank. I didn't see the big tank until they first started shooting in it. It was about a hundred times the size of the practice tank and it was so much deeper, so that was sort of scary when I first got there, because you have to get used to all the pressure and things like that. It is completely blue in there and there are divers with breathing equipment that are completely blue as well. You can't really see anything. You just get this breather put into your mouth after the take has been done. I got used to it quickly though.'

> '**I get on really well with Katie [Leung], she's a really cool girl… I dance with her, and there's a lot of scenes like holding hands and stuff like that.**'
> **– Robert Pattinson**

When discussing the film's Yule Ball scene, Robert cringed: 'I think the most embarrassing part of that was just the normal dancing. When the rock band comes. I think there was two days where the crew was like, "Just dance, just dance." But it's not like being in a club or whatever. That was really awkward.'

Cedric Diggory would meet an untimely end in the film, causing Robert's brief *Harry Potter* career to finish before it had flourished. Due to the death of such a prominent character, many fans saw this extension of the *Harry Potter* series as darker than its predecessors. Robert was quick to acknowledge that 'kids have followed the books quite closely, so the worry is this film is going to be dark for them.' But as he also quite rightly surmised: 'Your imagination is more terrifying than a film could ever be, and I think they're ready to see this side of the franchise.' His character's demise notwithstanding, he would return in a flashback scene for the next *Harry Potter* movie. Talking of his final death scene, where he is killed by Peter Pettigrew (Timothy Spall) and Lord Voldemort, Pattinson recalled, 'We redid it three times I think, because Ralph Fiennes could only shoot on certain days. So me and Dan tried to get bits of it done without him, and when he came – because of the way the last bits were shot with Voldermort – a lot of it had to be rearranged, and so it was strange because the first time I shot it I had about a month off through January, and so I sort of psyched myself up to do this scene, and then when we re-shot it I think we were filming the Yule Ball at the same time… it was exciting.'

The incessant action of the fourth *Harry Potter* movie was a veritable feast for fans all over the globe, and the steady, convincing performance of Robert as Cedric Diggory was a notable highlight of the film. In a movie filled with new and veteran talent alike, Pattinson's performance drew notable plaudits, and the *Times Online* were one of the greatest advocates of this bright young talent. They were quick to recognise Robert's potential and promptly named him 2005's 'British Star of Tomorrow'. The website said: 'This fresh-faced, photogenic eighteen-year-old so oozes charm and likeability that casting directors are predicting a big future.'

Variety magazine made a comment which Robert picked up on, necessitating a quick flick through the dictionary. 'I read the *Variety* review and their only comment was "rangy",' he remembered. 'I thought it meant from the range, like a cowboy. But it just means tall and lanky.' It was not only the media who were lavish in their praise of Robert Pattinson. By the time of the premiere for *Harry Potter And The Goblet Of Fire* Robert was becoming aware of the degree to which a role in a big movie can change your life instantaneously. 'I was in a trance the whole way through the premiere,' he remembered. 'The day before I was just sitting in Leicester Square, happily being ignored by everyone. Then suddenly strangers are screaming your name. Amazing.' For the premiere, Robert shunned designers by wearing a second-hand red velvet jacket that he'd purchased – like much of his wardrobe – from a charity shop.

'I hadn't done a film or a part that big before so it was interesting. Working with like the best actors in England, the most famous actors, it was really fun, really exciting.' – Robert Pattinson

His newfound fame was soon confirmed when he was stopped in the street for his first memorable signing session. 'Somebody asked for my autograph the other day,' a somewhat surprised Robert recalled. 'Because I finished school and I'm not really doing anything at the moment, I was just kind of aimlessly wandering around London, and these two guys who were about thirty came up and asked for my autograph. I was really quite proud at the time, and they wanted to take photos and stuff.'

Robert did, however, harbour secret doubts for future movie premieres, which was interesting given the furore that *Twilight* would soon cause. 'I've been to a couple of Warner Brothers film premieres in the last few weeks,' he said, 'and considering no one knows who I am, it's still a pretty scary event. So I don't know what it's gonna be like when you actually have to do something rather than just walk in. I still trip over my feet and stuff when I'm not supposed to be doing anything. So, I'll just see how it goes. I'm looking forward to it.'

Fans, casting agents, and directors expected Robert to take on a huge movie role imminently, but it was not going to pan out as they had all imagined.

Looking to the future: Robert at the Tokyo premiere of Harry Potter And The Goblet Of Fire, *November 2005.*

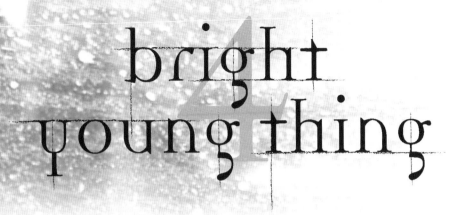

bright
young thing

'I realised I needed to learn some
of the fundamentals – like how to act.'
– Robert Pattinson

Showing a remarkable sense of perspective and legitimacy, Robert Pattinson had an
unpredictable reaction to his first successful major movie role. Admittedly, he had
not been the star of the film and it had not been a breakthrough performance – his
part was too limited for it to be so. Yet he had pulled off a tremendous feat in adapting
so smoothly to his new status as a top young actor. He'd performed alongside major
names and some personal heroes, and played his part as coolly as if he were still in a
back-room theatre in Barnes.

It was after *Harry Potter And The Goblet Of Fire* that Pattinson was first blessed with
the sobriquet of 'the next Jude Law', as Flora Stubbs revealed in the *London Evening
Standard* in November 2005. 'Robert Pattinson, nineteen, is being dubbed "the next Jude
Law" for a screen-stealing performance as the dashing head boy in *Harry Potter And The
Goblet Of Fire*. The London-born teenager, who plays Potter's love rival, will set hearts
racing among female cinema goers when the film is released this month.'

Naturally Stephanie Ritz, his agent from the US-based Endeavor Talent Agency, was
eager to line Robert up in another big-name, high-budget movie – a blockbuster in which
his potential would be realised and blast him into orbit. Pattinson, however, played up to
the archetype of his Taurus astrological sign and stubbornly denied all that came his way.
He had enjoyed *Harry Potter*, but not so much that he felt the need to jump into another
huge production for the sake of it.

Besides, money wasn't a pressing issue – he had been paid handsomely for his *Harry
Potter* appearance and decided to make use of the money by only taking on projects
which he deemed fulfilling. He also rented a flat in Soho with friend Tom Sturridge,
which he described as a 'cool little ex-crack den'. 'We spent the better part of a year just
getting drunk every night,' Robert recalled. 'It [the flat] was so cool. You had to walk
through a restaurant kitchen to get up to the roofs, but you could walk along all the

Following Harry Potter's *global publicity tour, Robert decamped to a rented flat in
London's Soho and 'spent the better part of a year just getting drunk every night'.*

In The Haunted Airman *(2006) Robert played Toby Jugg, a crippled World War Two pilot whose convalescence takes a disturbing psychological turn.*

roofs. I didn't do anything for a year, I just sat on the roof and played music, it was the best time I had ever had.'

Career-wise, Robert eventually settled on a London stage production and returned to tread the boards in familiar theatre grounds, accepting a role in an adaptation of a German play titled *The Woman Before*. This was going to be no easy task, as it was an experimental black comedy; one which may have lost something in the translation. Still, it was suitably 'arty' for Robert Pattinson. This was no cast of unknown thespians, however. Among the performers was Helen Baxendale (who had appeared in *Friends* and *Cold Feet* amongst many other television roles).

'At the time I really thought, "Wow, I must be great, I'm like fucking Brando!"' Pattinson joked of his move to theatre after such a high-profile film. 'I had this specific idea where "I'm going to be a weirdo, this is how I'm going to promote myself." And then of course I ended up getting fired.'

The exact reason for Pattinson's firing is not known, if indeed he was actually sacked. In other accounts of the run-up to the play's opening it is claimed that he pulled out shortly before the first performance. Either way he was replaced by Tom Riley, and set his sights on television once again. Whether Robert was sacked or voluntarily pulled out of the production, it was not the most sensible course of action towards establishing a career, and the question was: would it harm his future chances? At first it seemed that this may be the case, as the next couple of Pattinson appearances were in resolutely obscure productions.

It was all the more strange because Robert had been so mindful of his good fortune during the filming of *Harry Potter*. On set he continually carried a journal which he would write in daily. 'It was my diary, but it became more and more and more about requests to the "fates",' he later said cryptically. "'I will do this if you provide me with this." It sounds absolutely ridiculous, but I had so much faith in this little book. I remember one time I wrote, "Please don't give me all my luck now. Make it all stretch. I don't mind waiting. Make it stretch for seventy years.'"

If these were truly Pattinson's thoughts, he was going to take the hard road to success and continued good fortune. He seemed to be somewhat confused at this time, though defiant and still in possession of his usual good humour. As he told one befuddled interviewer, 'The acting's come along by accident. I've never trained or anything, so I've only very recently become even vaguely comfortable with it. On *Harry Potter* I was so conscious of the fact that I didn't know what I was doing. I used to sit on the side of the set throwing up. I think I will go to drama school now, though. I did a play which I got fired from in the West End, and I realised I needed to learn some of the fundamentals – like how to act.'

'My best acting experience was *The Haunted Airman* for BBC2. I play a World War Two pilot who gets shot and paralysed. He gets terrible shellshock and basically goes insane. It's a great part.' – Robert Pattinson

Robert only appeared in one role for the whole of 2006. *The Haunted Airman* was adapted from the 1948 Dennis Wheatley novel *The Haunting of Toby Jugg*, and directed by Chris Durlacher. Pattinson again starred alongside Julian Sands (from *Ring Of The Nibelungs*) and Rachael Stirling, who was an experienced television actress. The cast, like the budget, was small and the part was distinctly sombre.

The Haunted Airman centres on a pilot who has been crippled at war and is plagued by visions and terrifying dreams every day and night. He is sent to convalesce at a home in Wales under the gaze of his aunt and psychiatrist. Soon, however, he begins to suspect his psychiatrist does not have his best intentions at heart.

Robert played the role of the pilot Toby Jugg (with Sands as the psychiatrist) and spent the duration of filming confined to a wheelchair. 'I play a World War Two pilot who gets shot and paralysed,' Pattinson explained. 'He gets terrible shellshock and basically goes insane. It's a great part. I was in a wheelchair all the time, which is always good, just chain-smoking throughout the entire film.'

Robert's family in particular were thrilled by what they thought was a tactile and intuitive performance. In a review by *The Stage* Pattinson was lauded both for his portrayal and, predictably, his ravishing good looks. They wrote, 'All of the BBC's blue filters must have been requisitioned for *The Haunted Airman*, a very disturbing, beautifully made and satisfyingly chilling ghost story. Pattinson – an actor whose jaw line is so finely chiselled it could split granite – played the airman of the title with a perfect combination of youthful terror and world weary cynicism. Julian Sands provided creepy support as the oleaginous Doctor Barnes, with Rachael Stirling as the airman's solicitous and attentive aunt.'

Yet if *The Haunted Airman* was deemed obscure, Pattinson took further steps away

A floppy-fringed and fresh-faced Robert in British television comedy drama The Bad Mother's Handbook *(2007).*

from Hollywood's bright lights when he accepted an even less salubrious role in *The Bad Mother's Handbook*, a British television film that few can claim to have seen. There were no big name actors, and the production – adapted from the novel by Kate Long and released in February 2007 – went largely unnoticed by critics and viewers alike.

The Bad Mother's Handbook focuses on Charlotte Cooper, played by Holly Grainger. Charlotte gets unceremoniously dumped by her boyfriend only to find out she is pregnant. She then develops problems with both her mother and grandmother, but is blessed with the friendship of Daniel Gale, played by Robert. Gale is a shy young man who develops feelings for Charlotte, and becomes a supportive presence in her life while she deals with pregnancy and her unravelling family relationships. This comedy drama won plaudits amongst the small number of viewers who saw it, but was hardly going to propel Robert Pattinson to superstardom.

Far better for his career was the brief flashback resurrection of Cedric Diggory in 2007's *Harry Potter And The Order Of The Phoenix*. Obviously there was no additional filming for Robert to undertake given that his character had been murdered, but it kept Pattinson's name in the spotlight. Though he was still moving along at his own pace, with scant regard for the usual rules of building an acting career, Robert's reappearance in the *Harry Potter* saga was a reminder that he could be a huge star. Robert was indeed going to be a household name, but it would take a little while longer than it might have done, because he was always going to construct a career on his own terms.

'Rob definitely comes alive when the cameras roll. His performance is always heightened by pressure.' – *How To Be* director Oliver Irving

The next two parts Robert played were virtually unnoticeable on the radar, though his contribution to both was characteristically superb. First came *The Summer House*, an

Robert's real-life musical skills came in handy while filming the award-winning indie film How To Be *(2008).*

independent British film written by Ian Beck and directed by Daisy Gili. The plot is simple, involving Richard, a grovelling boyfriend played by Robert, following Jane (Talulah Riley) to France and trying to win back her love after being unfaithful. The film itself was unremarkable, though quaint, yet it was most revealing in terms of how casting agents were viewing Robert Pattinson.

According to the official notes for *The Summer House*, the character of Richard is 'a good-looking boy, with an ambivalent feminine side, skinny and androgynous in the fashion of that time'. He is also described as 'narcissistic' and termed 'the kind of boy who will hang around looking pitiful and hoping his moodiness will attract girls, which it does'.

Clearly Pattinson was viewed according to the specifications of his modelling portfolio – he even matched the 'androgynous' tag. Though he was able to play the role of Richard, it was evident that few casting agents were aware of his ultimate potential and diversity. His next part invoked a similar style, but at least this time Robert's promising talents would be noticed. For *How To Be* Robert was cast in the lead role of Art.

Director Oliver Irving remembered: 'Robert walked in to the audition and reminded me of people I know. I think he forgot his lines and just started improvising which is exactly what I wanted – someone who could just become the character and leave behind the kind of "techniques" trained in at drama schools. I had a hunch he would work well with [the] other cast [members] and would be able to get across the kind of naivety inherent to Art's character. He's a really down-to-earth guy

> **'My hair starts to wash itself. If you don't wash it for six weeks you won't have to wash it ever again. Until it gets unbearable.'**
> **– Robert Pattinson**

– it was funny because he told us he had a part in a *Harry Potter*, but as you can imagine, many actors in England have had tiny parts in those films. Plus, he really underplayed it, so I didn't think much of it at the time. It wasn't until we had cast him [that] I watched the *Harry Potter* film he was in and realised he was a major part.'

Having been dumped by his girlfriend, Robert's character Art moves in with his parents and persuades a Canadian self-help guru to travel to London and assist him in rebuilding his life. 'I love the script so much,' Robert revealed. '[It's] very different from everything I read. And the ending – I love it so much.'

The director was full of praise for Robert's portrayal of his character, gushing, 'Rob definitely comes alive when the cameras roll. His performance is always heightened by pressure – in rehearsals he would often say, "Okay, it's not right now, but I know what is needed and I'll get it on the day." This took an awful lot of faith in him but he was true to his word. He responds very well to direction and was also very up for contributing.'

Irving recalled one particularly memorable day of shooting: 'I remember when working on the first scene with him and Johnny White, who played Ronny, he [Robert] said to me, "I've seen these kind of relationships – two losers who wind each other up but still kind of rely on each other." He totally understood the dynamic. I remember he added the little line, "You're such an idiot," under his breath – the delivery of which really got the scene across for me, so I kept it in.'

How To Be featured a small cast and budget but garnered positive reviews from the mostly underground film buffs who saw it. Eventually, due to Robert's fame post-*Twilight*, certain media outlets would pick up on the movie. The likes of TMF, a subsidiary of MTV, were glowing in their praise of the picture, specifically Pattinson's performance.

'There are good things going for *How To Be*,' the TMF reviewer wrote. 'One is you get this feeling that the filmmakers and everyone involved did not do it for the money, but to give us a good story, with characters rich and funny and honest and, most of all, just like us. There are no heroes here, nor are we forced to make believe. And you'll get to see Robert Pattinson as an emerging actor with such potential – you will simply want to watch more and more of his films!'

It was ironic really. Here was Robert Pattinson playing small, understated roles – most recently as a bumbling lump in need of guidance – and yet all the while he was pleasing himself and furthering his career, whether or not he knew or even cared. By now he was achieving recognition on a wider scale, and it would not be long before his potential carried him to far greater things. Robert was awarded 'Best Actor 2008' at the Strasbourg Film Festival for his portrayal of Art in *How To Be*, and was ranked Number 23 on Moviefone's 'The 25 Hottest Actors Under 25'. Robert Pattinson was about to break through to the big time, but first he threw another curveball.

Creature of the night: Robert leaves London's Groucho Club with TV presenter Miquita Oliver (left) and an unnamed female friend in November 2007.

'I hope there is such a thing [as a soul mate]. I guess it would be quite scary to find a soul mate when you're young because you're probably going to mess it up.'
– Robert Pattinson

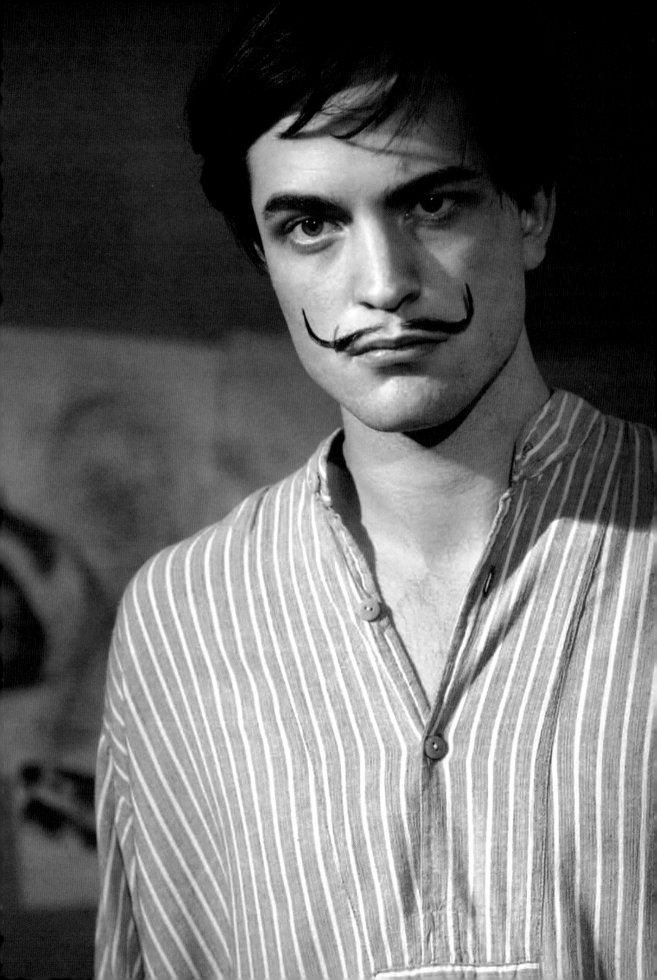

surreal life

'I did *Little Ashes* before *Twilight* and
I assume it will come out at some point next year.
It's a tiny, tiny movie, and I don't know what would have
happened if *Twilight* hadn't happened.'
– Robert Pattinson

After a smattering of arty, small-budget roles, Robert Pattinson was becoming disillusioned with the acting profession and considered turning to his other love, music. When asked why he was so disheartened, Robert would say, 'Mainly because when most films are being made now they're designing it to make money even before it's started shooting. Prejudging an audience is completely impossible to do. "Audiences bought this so they're going to like this." It's impossible to do. But you're going to make the same movie again and again. No one's going to break out of it. I just thought, "I don't want to be adding shit to the pile so I might as well complain about it and not be part of it."'

Of course, Robert was only apathetic towards the business side of acting rather than the art itself. Despite this reticence to bow down to the commercial aspects of filmmaking, he read the script for *Little Ashes*, a film based on the life of the surrealist painter Salvador Dali, and realised that this was exactly the kind of production he wanted to be involved with at this stage of his life.

Little Ashes – its title taken from one of Dali's paintings – was certainly intriguing, yet Robert almost ended up playing another character in the movie. 'I was attached to that for about, I guess, two years,' he said, 'and I was initially going to play Federico Garcia Lorca [Dali's friend and lover]. And somehow, I don't know what happened. They asked me to read for Dali, and that was about a year after. It took ages to get this film made. It was a really interesting script, and about a year after I was in mind for Lorca I read for Dali, and about a year after that they suddenly said, "Oh, we've got money, we're doing it in Spain, and it starts in four days!" So I came and I just thought it would be kind of fun, I mean, you know the stuff Dali makes, kind of crazy, and I thought it would be quite fun to do.'

Suddenly Robert became the main focus of the movie, and ended up having to immerse himself in heavy research. He felt that this was exactly the type of challenge which could keep him continually inspired. The prospect of spending months alone in

Robert as Salvador Dali in Little Ashes *(2008),
a biopic about the early life of the iconic surrealist painter.*

Spain, despite him not speaking a word of Spanish, did not dissuade him from the task.

The intensity of his research and the attention to detail he brought to the role was extremely rewarding, and it was the catalyst that would re-ignite his passion for acting. The nature of the low-budget film helped considerably. Despite its elaborate themes and multitude of actors, the movie cost a paltry £1.4 million to make – fifty-four times less than *Harry Potter And The Goblet Of Fire*.

'I couldn't speak to anyone the whole time,' Robert recalled. 'And so I just sat over this Dali stuff. I just read and read and read, and it was one of the most satisfying jobs I've ever done because it was the one time that I really had zero distractions. It really changed my whole attitude toward acting. And it was a tiny, tiny, film, which I don't think anyone will ever see, probably! But it was very interesting. Especially since I don't look anything like Dali. But at the end of the job, I kind of did look like him.'

Some people would have struggled to absorb the eccentricities and contradictions of the Catalan painter, yet Robert not only found these traits inspirational, he also seemed to find them quite amusing. 'When he was younger, if you read his autobiographical stuff – he wrote three autobiographies which completely contradict each other,' Pattinson said of Dali. 'There are chapters called "Truth" and other ones are called "Lies"… it's just really funny. There was so much about him that I found fascinating. He was an incredibly complex person. I'm not saying that I am. I'm not at all.'

> 'Playing Dali has been a complete turning point for me. It's the first part I've had that has required really serious thought. I became completely obsessed…'
> – Robert Pattinson

Though Robert played down his own complexities, it was likely he saw at least some of himself in Dali, if only in order to play the role so perfectly. 'I wasn't even really that big a fan of Dali's art,' he admitted. 'And even now, I kind of love the guy as a person. I mean, I find him fascinating, and in a really weird way I related to him a lot. And I appreciate his art a lot more, as with a lot of artists who are painters and stuff, I enjoy their art more once I know the sort of back story behind it. I don't know why, really.'

There were various convoluted aspects of the life and times of Salvador Dali, not least his full name, which was a tongue-twisting Salvador Domingo Felipe Jacinto Dali i Domènech, 1st Marquis of Púbol. He was born in Figueres in Catalonia, Spain, in 1904, and lived until he was eighty-four. Dali was predominantly known as a surrealist painter – a style of art which originated when he was still a teenager – but he is also noted for his contributions to theatre, fashion, photography and beyond. He once said, 'Every morning upon awakening, I experience a supreme pleasure: that of being Salvador Dali.'

There was a moment of light relief during the filming – though it could have potentially evolved into something far more sinister. 'I had a stalker while filming in Spain,' Robert later recalled. 'She stood outside of my apartment every day for weeks – all day, every day.' Revealing his secret method of counteracting potential fanatics, he explained: 'I was so bored and lonely that I went out and had dinner with her. I just complained about everything in my life and she never came back. People get bored of me, in like, two minutes.'

Little Ashes featured a mostly Spanish cast, aside from the inclusion of the odd British actor, notably the up-and-coming, Manchester-based Matthew McNulty (who had recently appeared in Anton Corbijn's acclaimed Joy Division biopic *Control*). The film follows the path of an eighteen-year-old Dali as he travels to early 1920s Madrid. There he moves into the Residencia de Estudiantes and meets filmmaker Luis Buñuel and poet Federico Garcia Lorca. He experiments with art, and his friendship with Lorca soon turns to love.

The visual aspect of the character was the principle area Pattinson needed to conquer – it was vital that Pattinson could mimic Dali's mannerisms, and so he pored over old photographs of the artist.

'I had this whole series of photos,' he said. 'And figured out the way he would move his body. There's a picture of him pointing. I spent days trying to figure out, "How did he get his arm like that?" It was the first time that I ever really got into characterisation, trying to work on movements. I was doing tons of stuff on his walk and such. It was probably unnecessary, but it was the one time I felt, like, slightly satisfied. But I wanted to bring that intensity to every job.'

Much of the interest in *Little Ashes* would be fuelled by Robert's appearance in *Twilight* and the subsequent eruption of his fame. At the time he filmed his parts for Dali, it remained a small-scale movie made with a fierce sense of independence.

'It was a very small film,' he said, 'but the more I read about him, the more I liked him. I wasn't really a fan of Dali before, but I tried, I worked harder than I've worked on anything for that because playing a real person it's like, you don't want to insult them, I guess… It's so different playing a real person than playing someone else. It made me learn a lot about how to research and look deeper into scripts 'cause it was such a complicated character, but I was really glad I did it.'

Nevertheless, Robert was aware that Dali was a multi-faceted exhibitionist, who could go from being an extroverted genius to an awkward introvert within the space of a day. The nature of surrealist painting may have given people certain opinions of Dali, and due to his frequently bizarre behaviour he was famed for his extreme eccentricity. But there was another side to his character: though Dali was considered straight, certainly in his youth, his gay relationship with Federico Garcia Lorca formed a substantial part of the movie. Though it would be a year before people latched onto the fact that Robert Pattinson had appeared in a gay love scene, when they did it was a controversial topic of discussion.

> 'I was so disillusioned before *Little Ashes* that I was going to give up acting, mainly because most movies being made now are designed in such a way that it's all about making a lot of money… I'd rather just not be a part of it.'
> – Robert Pattinson

Dali often confirmed he was straight, and with reference to Lorca he repeatedly claimed that he had rejected the older poet's advances. Dali was recorded as saying of Lorca, 'He was homosexual, as everyone knows, and madly in love with me... I was extremely

Photographed by KEVIN FOORD

A surreal career

Robert Pattinson, who played Hogwarts' wholesome head boy, has been picked to portray Salvador Dalí as a sexually ambiguous young man. **Emily Bearn** meets a youth in a hurry to grow up

Love, art, betrayal: Javier Beltran and Robert undertook months of intensive research to bring their characters' complex relationship to life onscreen.

annoyed, because I wasn't homosexual, and I wasn't interested in giving in... So nothing came of it.' Director Paul Morrison said of the movie's more risqué moments: 'Sex scenes are always difficult to shoot, uncomfortable and technically difficult because you're dealing with something that is very personal and intimate, so you need that emotion but you also have to reduce it.' He cryptically added: 'We weren't paying the actors enough to reveal too much.'

Philippa Goslett, the writer of *Little Ashes*, spoke out in justification of including the Dali-Lorca affair. 'Having done a huge amount of research, it's clear something happened, no question,' she stated. 'When you look at the letters it's clear something more was going on there. It began as a friendship, became more intimate and moved to a physical level, but Dali found it difficult and couldn't carry on.'

Robert Pattinson's skilful handling of a difficult role – not least the gay relationship –

puts him in line with other big-name Hollywood stars who have played gay characters, Heath Ledger and Will Smith among them. It was merely another string to the Pattinson bow, and one which would garner him acclaim.

Ultimately the Dali role became his saviour. It fired his passion for acting once again and revealed that the business still boasted plenty of serious filmmakers and actors who cared more about their art than financial gain or their own hunger for fame. The fact that he impressed those he was working alongside enhanced his career further still. As Carlo Dusi, executive producer of *Little Ashes*, would later say, 'Robert Pattinson was as friendly, approachable and fun to be around in our downtime as he was a true professional while on set, and his commitment to becoming Salvador Dali was extremely impressive – and paid off in generating a performance which I personally think is extraordinary.'

Robert also succeeded in undoing any possibility of being typecast. He smartly observed that if he was to have a rewarding, long-term career he had to take on daring, challenging roles that appealed to him, and avoid the easy route that would have led to quicker fortune but potential discontent.

'I wasn't really a fan of Dali before, but I tried, I worked harder than I've worked on anything... I was really glad I did it.' – Robert Pattinson

'I didn't want to get stuck in pretty, public-school roles, or I knew I'd end up as some sort of caricature,' he revealed. 'Playing Dali has been a complete turning point for me. It's the first part I've had that has required really serious thought. I became completely obsessed with Dali during the filming. He was the most bizarre, complex man, but in the end I felt I could relate to him. He was basically incredibly shy.'

Though Robert finished filming *Little Ashes* well before his appearance in *Twilight*, the promoters behind the biopic sensibly took advantage of Pattinson's rising star by releasing his Dali portrayal in the UK and USA in 2009. However, the film did appear at the Raindance Film Festival in October 2008, and that same month was also screened at the Valladolid Film Festival in Spain. A writer for the festival observed: 'While it is a far cry from his role in the *Harry Potter* franchise, Robert Pattinson brings Dali to the screen with precisely the irreverent and eccentric personality you would expect from one of the creators of Spain's avant-garde movement.'

Robert Pattinson had pulled away from the big-budget Hollywood set even before he'd permanently established himself within it. Yet his aversion to high-profile fame was about to be seriously tested as his career took an extraordinary turn once again.

live forever

'I'd read the fan sites after my screen test,
and I'd never even heard of the books before. And when
we were doing the movie, then they got exponentially bigger
and bigger and bigger and then everybody knew about it.
So it was strange, unexpected.'
– Robert Pattinson

Though Robert Pattinson was perfectly content to perform small-scale roles and develop his skills to his own satisfaction, his agency were still working on breaking him into the big time. Yet even when Robert was steered along the appropriate path he seemed reluctant to bow down to the powers that be. 'I got sent to media training and my agent got back messages like, "He's resisting the media training,"' he laughed.

Robert had not set the world on fire as Cedric Diggory by any means, but his appearance in the film showed potential casting agents that he had the ability to take to the big screen in a huge-budget Hollywood movie, and do so without difficulty. Robert's résumé was plied not only around the desks of numerous high-profile movie executives, but anywhere else where there seemed to be potential.

The role of Edward Cullen in a movie adaptation of Stephenie Meyer's novel *Twilight* seemed to be one such avenue for growth. The initial novel was eventually followed by three sequels, and *The Twilight Saga* – as the series was known – became so successful that production on a long-rumoured movie based on the first book finally began. Known as a 'vampire romance' novel, *Twilight* was originally published in 2005. It told the story of seventeen-year-old Isabella 'Bella' Swan, who moves from Arizona to the small rain-soaked town of Forks, Washington to live with her father when her mother remarries. Bella has always felt isolated and socially awkward, and doesn't expect anything to change when she moves to Forks. But her life does indeed change, in an extraordinary fashion.

She meets the beautiful, intelligent and charismatic Edward Cullen, a seventeen-year-old who carries a dark secret. Almost instantly she feels Cullen is her soul-mate, and they are swept into a romance which is unorthodox to say the least, for Edward is a vampire who was born in 1901 but has retained the appearance of a seventeen-year-old. He can run faster than a mountain lion, read minds, and stop a speeding car with his bare hands. He is also, of course, immortal. However, unlike other fictional vampires, he does not

Robert breaks hearts – and box-office records
– as 'vegetarian' vampire Edward Cullen.

drink human blood, he can withstand normal light, and he doesn't possess a pair of razor-sharp fangs. Robert mused on his character's supernatural abilities:

'Once you decide to play something you just have to say, "Okay, these are the facts of the character," and you just have to commit to a belief in them. You're reading minds. I mean, he's reading minds the entire time. So I kind of was trying to get that into my head. Most of the time it's just a question of humanising it. It's every little aspect, like, how would you as an individual react or behave and think if, for instance, you were one thousand times stronger than any other human being or one thousand times faster and it suddenly comes out of nowhere. You just normalise everything. And that's kind of what I try and do. Just make it relatable to some aspect of yourself.'

Robert was complimentary regarding Stephenie Meyer's desire to avoid the usual vampire clichés. 'Luckily, Stephenie didn't have vampire lore in the book,' he explained. 'It's very specific, and the characters in the book even kind of joke about the mythology about vampires, and so you can kind of get another element of realism there. I think it also makes it more frightening, and that's what I liked about Catherine Hardwicke directing it, because I went into it thinking

'Twilight takes a lot of teenage life and emotion extremely seriously and in a non-ironic way.'
– Robert Pattinson

it's going to be shot with this kind of realism and grittiness, and I thought that could work for this story. I mean, it's trying to reinvent the vampire genre a bit.'

Kristen Stewart, who was cast as Bella, was drawn towards *Twilight* 'because vampires are classically meant to draw you in to the point where they have you in a complete submitting state to where they can then kill you'.

Robert also believed the *Twilight* phenomenon blended into the most obvious 'outsider' culture of modern times. 'It has always been associated with Goth culture,' he said, 'and it's become more mainstream, so everybody seems to be an emo now. I think it's because young people feel like they don't connect with anything anymore. There's no such thing as an insider anymore. I think everybody feels like outsiders and I think vampires are really the definition of them. I mean, anyone who preys on the rest of humanity is obviously going to be an outsider to society, so I guess that's why it is.'

Edward, like the rest of the Cullens, drinks animal rather than human blood, but warns Bella her life may be in danger if she stays with him – he still feels the need to kill her, despite his love. 'The relationship between the characters is kind of like Edward goes, "Every day, I really want to kill you, you don't understand," and Bella goes, "I don't care, I love you!"' Robert later said. 'I guess the whole thing is that you can only have that kind of love story when you're young and you're sort of overcome by your emotions and it seems so life-or-death.'

As the story unfolds, we learn that Bella is in danger from a far greater threat than her beloved Edward. Cullen must protect Bella from James (played by Cam Gigandet in the movie); a vampire who is hell-bent on killing her and drinking her blood. Thus, Edward becomes locked in a battle with the violent and calculating predator.

Three thousand young male actors sent their résumés in for the role of Edward – and many were given the chance to audition. Stephenie Meyer had a huge hand in deciding who would play the role of Cullen, and she – along with director Catherine Hardwicke (who had directed *Thirteen* and *Lords Of Dogtown*) – pored over a huge book of headshots to find the personification of the fictional vampire.

'It was a massive challenge to find Edward,' said Hardwicke. 'Not many actors can live up to the image in the book – the pale skin and the otherworldly beauty.' She said most of the actors who had tried to become Edward Cullen 'were handsome but they all looked like the All-American guy. Pattinson was different; he had everything we needed and he had that angular face and kind of mysterious Edward aura.'

'My agent started wearing a "Team Edward" badge.' – Robert Pattinson

In Meyer's view the candidate needed to carry both the charm and fear factor. 'We needed someone who was both pretty and scary,' she said. 'The one guy that kids were always saying they wanted for Edward was Tom Welling from *Smallville*. He's beautiful! But could you ever imagine being afraid of him? We did not have a good option until Rob came along. And the movie rests entirely on his shoulders.'

Once Robert had been confirmed as Edward, Stephenie Meyer spoke with satisfaction on hearing the news. 'I am ecstatic with Summit's choice for Edward,' she said. 'There are very few actors who can look both dangerous and beautiful at the same time, and even fewer who I can picture in my head as Edward. Robert Pattinson is going to be amazing.'

Kristen Stewart concurred. 'Not to put down any of the other actors who came in,' she said, 'because they were really good, but everyone came in playing Edward as this perfect, happy-go-lucky guy, but I got hardcore pain from Rob. It was purely just connection.'

Robert knew little of the back story, or the potential of the series. His primary concern was avoiding a cheesy teen adaptation. 'I didn't want to do a stupid teen movie,' he said. 'Even little kids don't want to hear you say the same pat stuff, it's boring! I'm thinking about my career in the long-term, rather than just trying to milk one thing for whatever it's worth. I specifically hadn't done anything which anyone would see since *Harry Potter*, because I wanted to teach myself how to act. I didn't want to be an idiot. *Twilight* came kind of randomly, and I didn't really know what it was when it first started. I wanted to do two or three more little things and then do something bigger, and then this kind of happened and I was like, "Well, okay."'

Had Robert known exactly the kind of furore and infamy this role would create he may well have thought twice. In many ways he underestimated the level of interest in the movie adaptation, though he was certainly aware of the book once he decided to audition. 'I was living in England and it wasn't big there,' he said of the *Twilight* book. 'I actually tried to read it five months before when somebody had told me about it, and I read a few pages, and I thought, "Oh, this isn't my thing." And I didn't know that there was a phenomenon. I thought it was a little bit "girly". But then I read the script and it cut out a lot of the descriptions... It read more like an action script. So later, I went back to the book and saw what the differences had been. I looked at it a bit more objectively.

I liked the book better when I came back to it the second time.'

Edward Cullen's physical perfection in the book created a certain amount of unease for young Robert Pattinson, who didn't quite feel comfortable performing the role of Mr Perfect. 'I was embarrassed even going into the audition,' he said. 'I thought I'd be judged. Anyone who turns up, you look on the synopsis of Edward and you see "Edward is the perfect man. He has an impeccable face, body. Everything about him is amazing," and even turning up for the audition is, like, "Hey, here I am!" It's so stupid, so I was quite happy when the reaction from the fans was a hundred percent negative. I was like, "Thank you. I'm not perfect. I'm rugged." All the blogs were, like, "He's a bum." I was like "Cool! I guess I'm going to be a character actor."'

Though most actors are inevitably nervous before auditions, one may have suspected Robert Pattinson of being slightly apathetic. By his own admission, he had no inkling of how he should approach the role, nor did he think he would succeed, but his *Twilight* audition induced a certain amount of trepidation.

> 'Edward's described as this perfect man,
> with an impeccable face and body. Everything about him is just
> amazing. There's no way I could ever live up to that.'
> – Robert Pattinson

'I went in having no idea how to play the part at all,' Robert recalled, 'and thinking there was no chance of getting it. I mean, Catherine literally didn't say anything during the whole audition. She just filmed. And Kristen did it so differently to how I was expecting Bella to be played that it kind of shocked a performance out of me. And it was the first time in a long time that I'd had an organic experience in an audition. And I thought that there could be a lot of depth to the story. But I only realised in the audition.'

Pattinson flew to Hardwicke's home in Venice, California for his audition, and it was not until this initial trial was underway that his desire to play the part of Edward became genuine. When he saw the intimacy with which he was being invited to play the role it spurred him on, albeit with yet more apprehension. After reading two scenes Catherine Hardwicke surprised Robert with a proposal – he had to conduct a love scene, on the director's own bed, no less. He was reading alongside Kristen Stewart, who had already been confirmed as Bella. 'Then we just make out and I try and kill her,' Robert recalled. 'It was funny. When I got into bed with Kristen I said, "I've only known you for an hour and we are in bed." I think I must have gone way over the top with it as well, because I remember looking up afterwards and Catherine Hardwicke had a look on her face as if to say, "What are you doing? You look like you're having a seizure!"'

Hardwicke was resolutely impressed, however, later stating the scene 'was electric. The room shorted out, the sky opened up, and I was like, "This is going to be good."'

Kristen Stewart was generous in her praise for the Londoner, saying, 'Rob came into the audition looking sort of terrified, like a subdued fear and pained. The pain was just very evident in him. I am not saying it's in Rob, but he knew what to bring to that

Above: Hungry eyes: The bloodthirsty Edward resists his primal urges.
Below: Bella (Kristen Stewart) and Edward tentatively begin their romance.

Too cool for school: Robert effortlessly evokes what Twilight *director Catherine Hardwicke called a 'mysterious Edward aura'.*

character. We didn't need the statuesque, model-types who come in and just pose. I couldn't see any of the other guys. They weren't even looking at me. It was like they were focusing on their lines, but Rob is very organic. He's in the moment and he lets it happen, which is brave. He's brave. He's a courageous actor.'

Director Catherine Hardwicke was more than satisfied that she had the perfect pair of actors to portray Edward and Bella. She spoke with admiration for Pattinson and Stewart, saying, 'I do feel lucky directing Kristen and Rob, because their faces are so beautiful. They're expressive. Their skin is just porcelain, and sometimes I am literally watching the monitor and I'm going, "Oh, I'm so excited!" just jumping up and down. But I don't want to say anything, because I want to keep them in the moment. Sometimes I feel like I'm getting gold here. And it is very exciting.'

Robert had to adopt an American accent for the role, but felt at ease with the dialect. 'I didn't have a coach or anything,' he said. 'American's fine, but I've never really been a big one for accents. Whenever I try to do any accents it ends up being a sort of Jamaican-Russian hybrid.' By the time of his audition Robert was very familiar with the role of Edward and his tempestuous relationship with Bella. But he was surprised, after absorbing the content of the novel, to realise the power balance between the two differed within the movie script. Robert felt the roles were somewhat reversed. He was supposed to be the strong one, yet he felt more strength of character from Kristen.

As Kristen had already been confirmed as Bella she had read alongside several actors who were auditioning for the role of Edward. As a consequence, Robert felt she may have been a little 'jaded'. This dynamic seemed to work from the beginning, despite Pattinson feeling uncomfortable in many ways.

'I think she'd done about ten readings that day,' Robert said of Kristen. 'I was kind of intimidated by what she was doing. I was stunned because it was so different from what I was expecting. And I guess it never really changed the whole way through, which kind of works, just in terms of the story, me having to be the powerful one but being intimidated by her. The relationship [was] built from that…We really weren't trying to act like we were in love with each other right from the beginning. It was more about trying to intimidate each other and showing how much we didn't care about the other person, which I guess worked. In a lot of ways that's how long-lasting relationships work.'

The equilibrium of the onscreen relationship seemed to be more natural than the one portrayed in the novel. Most strikingly of all, the book's implication of Bella being a meek, mild damsel was obliterated by the strength which Kristen Stewart conveyed. Perhaps it was a natural characteristic, or perhaps it came from her having had a lengthy career at such a young age. Though Stewart was only born in 1990, by the time she came to work on *Twilight* she had already acted in sixteen different television and movie roles, starring alongside the likes of Jodie Foster and Forest Whitaker in *Panic Room* and Samuel L. Jackson in *Jumper*. Stewart was a seasoned young actress and able to play Bella as hopelessly in love, but with a commendable strength.

> 'Rob is very organic. He's in the moment and he lets it happen which is brave. He's brave. He's a courageous actor.'
> – Kristen Stewart

'Kristen is very strong,' Robert confirmed. 'Just naturally, she's not the kind of damsel in distress at all. So just reading it without comparing that at all, it made me realise the kind of a balance that Edward has with her. It made it easier to portray. It makes much more sense, when the relationship is with someone you can rely on... I really didn't expect the girl who's playing Bella to be that strong when I went in.'

Aside from their respective roles Robert also felt an instant kinship with Kristen because of her personal strength, noting, 'She doesn't back down to people. And it was quite good working with her, for me, because I don't like backing down to people.'

After Robert was confirmed for the role of Edward Cullen he set about embracing his part – a little too seriously, some thought. He travelled alone to Portland, Oregon, where he would prepare for two months before the remainder of the cast and the crew joined him. Oregon, in the north-west of the United States, was chosen due to its often overcast climate. However, the cast and crew would eventually have to deal with changeable weather, which often included sunshine – not what the producers wanted whilst creating a dark vampire movie.

'Oregon has the strangest weather stuff that happens,' Robert said, 'especially in the spring when we were shooting. It would be like sunny, snowing, raining, and hailing at the exact same time.' One day, after filming had begun, all who were on set endured snow, rain, and hail. 'There were some days I cried,' said Catherine Hardwicke. 'But then I would see these girls and mums who loved the book standing in the rain watching, and I'd think, "I can't have a pity party. I better stand up and make this scene great. I don't care if it is hailing on me."'

Robert read the *Twilight* script relentlessly and was also privy to a copy of *Midnight Sun*, a Stephenie Meyer novel which is yet to be published. It recounts the events of *Twilight*, but is written from Edward Cullen's perspective. According to Meyer, the manuscript needs to be rewritten before it's made available to the public. '*Midnight Sun* didn't really influence my performance,' Pattinson ventured, 'I always found that girls are more attracted to the dangerous, the wrong. And so I wanted to put in as much of the dangerous factor of Edward's state into the performance. He's very tightly wound in a lot of places and also there's a fury inside him, and a rage which he has very, very little control over. A lot of which was in *Midnight Sun*. The only thing that I really needed to know was the extent of reaction when he first met Bella, which was in the first chapter. When he was very much

'When I was first cast everybody hated me, universally... That was my welcome to *Twilight*.'
– Robert Pattinson

considering killing her – he's weighing up the option of killing the entire school just so that he can kill her and there's no witnesses. And he said that, he's not saying it like it's a very distant possibility, he has to make his mind up about the whole situation in a matter of seconds. I kind of want to put that more into the performance.'

As Pattinson felt his own performance being influenced by his co-star, so he attempted to impress and influence her. 'In the beginning I thought to myself, "Because she's so serious, I've got to be really serious,"' he said. 'I didn't speak for about two months so I would seem really intense. I would only ever talk about the movie. And I kept recommending all these books. It didn't really work, though. Then I started falling apart and my character started breaking down. I felt like an idiot just following her around, saying, "You really should read some Zola – and there's this amazing Truffaut movie." And she started calling me on things: "Have you actually watched this movie? Yeah? What's it about?" "It's about a guy on a train." "Did you just look at the photo on the cover of the DVD?"'

On a physical level, Robert felt the need to mimic Edward Cullen's perfect body as it's described in *Twilight*. This meant during the two months spent alone in Oregon, Pattinson regularly spent long hours in a local gym, toughening up and developing an impressive physique. It went a little too far, however, as he recalled. 'Three weeks before shooting the producers were like, "What are you doing? You look like an alien!" Oh, well, I thought it was a cool idea.' *Entertainment Weekly* reported that Robert had over-exercised to such a degree that his penance was to lay off the gym work and overindulge in cheeseburgers instead. 'I literally stopped exercising,' Robert recalled. 'Eating a cheeseburger after two and a half months of doing that – it tasted like ambrosia.'

Robert may have had the wrong idea about his character's physical prowess, but his headshots would come back to haunt him when the producers decreed that his smile

Edward is torn between Bella's love and his need for her blood.

'Twilight is a Romeo and Juliet love story.'
– Catherine Hardwicke

was not quite perfect enough for the movie-going public. He had some expensive dental work and was forced to wear a brace afterwards. 'They wanted me to have the perfect smile,' Robert explained. 'I never thought anything was wrong with my teeth. But the producers still wanted me to wear a brace.'

He also had to wear contact lenses in order to give Edward the required liquid gold look. This was particularly uncomfortable for Robert, who later said, 'I have very sensitive eyes, so it took like twenty minutes to get in the contacts every single day. People said you get used to it after awhile, but after three and a half months, it never, ever got better. It also limits you… it's like you have these masks on your eyes, which take away the life from them, which is very frustrating sometimes. You just have to be shot and look like you're expressionless.'

Robert persisted in his work – complete with expensive dental brace – without complaint, and instead pondered the difficulties of portraying Edward Cullen's beauty alongside his venomous impulses. 'That was the thing in the book, the key thing was that he be attractive,' he said. 'And it was especially challenging when you're trying to be frightening and pretty at the same time. It's quite a complicated scenario, especially when you have to stay PG-13.'

love bites

7

'There was a huge, universal backlash about my being cast as Edward Cullen. Seventy-five thousand *Twilight* fans signed a petition against me. But, I mean, I expected it.'
– Robert Pattinson

When the filming for *Twilight* finally began it was clear Robert Pattinson had perhaps over-involved himself with the character of Edward, at least as director Catherine Hardwicke and co-star Kristen Stewart saw it. Two months of solid research and detailed character construction had, by all accounts, rendered Robert an over-analytical grump. It may have caused his co-stars and crew to be concerned about his state of mind, but Robert felt it necessary to experience the world through Edward Cullen's eyes, even going so far as to write a journal in character. 'I wanted to feel his isolation,' he said dryly.

In an attempt to lighten Robert's mood, the producers trailed behind him on set highlighting passages from the book where Edward actually smiled. 'It was like, "Argh! I was going to smile at some point,"' Robert recalled. 'Or everyone would be like, "Well, let's try to make this bit funnier!" But it wasn't funny. I tried to play it, as much as possible, like a seventeen-year-old boy who had this purgatory inflicted on him. I just thought, "How would you play this part if it wasn't a teen book adaptation?"'

Kristen Stewart also seemed to find it amusing that Robert could not distinguish between the angst of the role and his own persona when the cameras were off. 'I had this little thing,' she said, '"Rob, let's just rehearse the scene all the way through without tearing it down and criticising it." We'd get two lines out, and then he would say, "No, no, no, it's not working!" Rob made himself crazy the whole movie, and I just stopped and patted him on the back through his neuroses. He would punch me in the face if he heard me right now.'

Still, the manner in which he should play Edward was an ongoing concern for Robert, and a responsibility he did not take lightly. He debated with Stephenie Meyer for many hours over how Edward should be portrayed in the movie versus how he is portrayed in the novel. 'I was talking to Stephenie Meyer saying, "The guy must be chronically

Robert and Kristen during a promotional photo shoot
at the Rome International Film Festival, October 2008.

depressed,"' Robert explained, 'and she was saying, "No, he's not, he's not, he's not." But I still maintain that he was. I mean, it's not like depressed, but just this sort of loneliness. I mean, when you see him at school he doesn't really talk to anyone. He must get bored after a while, only hanging out with the same four people in his life.'

Subsequent reports suggested Pattinson and Meyer 'fell out' over the discrepancy, but the two merely sought to create the best Edward possible, with maximum deference to the original story. 'With Rob, we sat down and talked about Edward's character before the filming started,' Stephenie clarified. 'It wasn't an argument, but we [did] actually disagree on his character. I'd be like, "No, this is how it is." He's like, "No, it's definitely this way." Yet in the performance he did what he wanted, and yet it was exactly what I wanted.'

> 'He's a vampire, he's a social pariah. He's not a role model. He's a parasite. That's the cool thing about it. I don't think a vampire has any responsibility to anybody.'
> – Robert Pattinson

Robert recalled he 'was trying to establish whether Edward would stay at the mentality of a seventeen-year-old, and I think that's kind of what he did. You can have as many experiences as you want, but if you're still in the mind of a seventeen-year-old, it must be very frustrating. Or having the world still see you as a kid when you're not a kid any more. Things like that. I think that a lot of how people mature is just the rest of the world treating you like an older person, not just living a long time. Because he knows he essentially is still seventeen, in most ways, and at the same time he's not.'

Robert saw Edward Cullen as a vulnerable character and played him accordingly. This was a careful balancing act, based on the notion that Bella was often in danger and that, coupled with Edward's need to be a fully functional human, created a distinct helplessness to the character.

'When his life is put into basic terms, he has nothing to live for and all he wants to do is either become a human or die,' Robert said. 'The only reason that he hasn't died is because he is too scared; he doesn't think that he has a soul. Then he meets Bella, who makes him feel like a human and feel alive again. At the same time, her human vulnerability makes him incredibly vulnerable, because even with his super speed and his super strength, he still can't fully protect her. Whenever she is in danger, he is in danger. If she dies or goes anywhere, then he is gone, too.'

Further ruminating on the sacrifices made by Bella and the implications of this for Edward, Robert mused: 'What I always thought was really interesting about Bella is that Edward doesn't really have a choice in how he chooses to love and to live, but Bella's choosing to give up her life, to give up her mortality, which is also something I found very strange about it. I mean, it is essentially how much she wants to be with Edward, but at the same time she has so little regard for remaining human, and they've only known each other for about, what, eight weeks or something? Is that how long the entire story's set? I mean, I don't know, and she's already saying, "I don't want to be a human any more after that!" I mean, that's what love is. I always thought Bella's character was really interesting.'

Blood feud: Edward prepares to do battle with the murderous James.

'It was a massive challenge to find Edward. Not many actors can live up to the image in the book – the pale skin and the otherworldly beauty… Pattinson was different; he had everything we needed and he had that angular face and kind of mysterious Edward aura.'
– *Twilight* director, Catherine Hardwicke

Despite Robert's obsessiveness and desire to create the perfect onscreen interpretation of Edward Cullen, the announcement that he had been cast as the revered vampire lover met with stern disapproval. At that time *Twilight* had been read by millions of readers around the world – seventeen million to be precise. There were casual readers of course, and those in between, but the *Twilight* covens who had long been looking forward to seeing Edward come to life on the big screen were initially mortified that a virtually unknown English actor had been picked. One report claimed that Robert's mother Clare read online that her only son was 'wretched and ugly' and 'had the face of a gargoyle'. This led Stephenie Meyer, who knew the extent of her readers' *Twilight* obsession, to apologise to Robert, albeit with her tongue-in-cheek, and a touch belatedly. 'I apologised to Rob, for ruining his life. There is going to be a group of girls who will follow his actions from now on. I asked the producer, "Is Rob ready for this? Have you guys prepped him? Is he ready to be the 'It Guy'?" I don't think he really is. I don't think he sees himself that way. And I think the transition is going to be a little rocky.'

Catherine Hardwicke also experienced the darker side of fan obsession, and explained how she was stopped in the street by *Twilight* readers of all ages. 'Everybody has such an idealised vision of Edward,' she said. 'They were rabid about who I was going to cast. Like, old ladies saying, "You better get it right."' As it happened, Meyer would be justified in questioning Robert's acceptance of mass fan adulation or ridicule. Pattinson shrugged off the initial verbal barbs, quipping, 'I stopped reading after I saw the signatures saying, "Please, anyone else."'

It didn't seem to matter to the producers of the movie, however, who no doubt saw any publicity as beneficial to promoting the film. Equally, the uncertainty and outright refusal of some to accept Robert as Edward Cullen still fuelled a latent curiosity as to whether he could pull it off. Furthermore, it was not only a reticence to accept Pattinson as Edward Cullen; uncertainty always hovers over movie renditions of novels, and the film rarely depicts what each reader subjectively imagines.

Nevertheless, Robert quickly learned how the readers expected Edward to come to life. 'What I never really understood about his attractiveness, especially to young girls, is his gentlemanliness,' he admitted. 'I thought that teenage girls like the dangerous aspect of males, and so I tried to emphasise the danger and make the more gentlemanly side of this character a veil to something else underneath. I really tried to make him an incredibly strong and powerful character, but at the same time self-loathing and extremely vulnerable.'

There were many memorable moments for Robert during shooting, some of which provided light relief from his obsessive dedication to remain in character at all times. Robert's favourite scene was one of the fiercest. 'I knew that there were some scenes where I was going to have to look demonic and have a glare that would scare humans,' he explained. 'That was difficult to prepare. My favourite scene that we ended up shooting was this little random one near the beginning where I try and intimidate Bella by being a scary vampire and she doesn't back down at all.'

Perhaps the scary aspect of Robert's character was never going to quite work considering his hairstyle. As he quipped,

'If Edward doesn't feel something one-hundred percent, he wouldn't bother trying to pretend to anyone that he does. I guess I'm similar to him in that respect.'
– Robert Pattinson

'You know, just the whole thing, having a bouffant haircut and stuff – it's not really that intimidating.' More memorable for the cast and crew were Robert's attempts to play baseball. Thankfully, it was only for one scene, but Edward Cullen is supposed to be perfectly comfortable on the baseball diamond, an alien concept to Robert Pattinson. The young actor couldn't help but be amused by the sporting focus of the scene. As he said with a chuckle, 'I'm terrible. I'm completely mal-coordinated. I'm terrible at all sports. Also, I don't see the point as well. I even had a baseball coach. Catherine was so determined to make me look like a professional baseball player, and I literally couldn't take it seriously.'

Above: *Edward looks on as the Cullen family's game of vampire baseball attracts some unwelcome visitors.*
Below: *'You're faster than the others, but not stronger.' James (Cam Gigandet) gets to grips with Edward.*

Though he would initially attempt his own stunts, Robert was soon persuaded that this wasn't the best course of action. And he left the *Twilight* set with a supreme admiration for those in the stunt business. 'I did quite a few of them,' he said proudly. 'But I had a good stunt double as well. He's a professional free runner. I can do something and get injured and look like crap playing it or he can do it and make it look really good and no one notices the difference. After a while, I tried to do the Tom Cruise thing, but I eventually gave up. But I did a whole bunch of it. I managed to pick up so many injuries whenever I tried the simplest of stunts. I went to pick up Kristen and I almost ripped my hamstring. It's not even a stunt. I literally did one squat. And this was after three months of training.'

> **'I think it's because vampires are classically meant to draw you in to the point where they have you in a complete submitting state to where they can then kill you. So that's a little bit sexy, to completely let something take over. It's forbidden fruit. It's something you can't have, you just want more.'**
> **– Kristen Stewart**

Far from being a primadonna, Robert was perfectly able to accept criticism or persuasion to do something differently in order to please the producers and the director. And it seemed that they had no reservations about telling their main actor exactly what to do, or whether to rework a particular scene. Catherine Hardwicke was especially blunt, though Robert responded admirably. 'She's such a free spirit,' he said of the *Twilight* director. 'She has no filter. She kind of gets you out of nowhere. Like she'd go, "You know that thing you're doing there? Yeah, that. That's not good." And I'd go, "Really?" And she'd say, "Yeah. It's weird. And it's not working. At all." The diplomacy department is not her finest. But you love that about her, that she feels free to say, "That sucked. Try something else." She wouldn't say I "sucked" but she'd go, "That's too big, too over the top. Try something subtler," which is really her way of saying that you sucked.'

To many people who have only recently been exposed to the *Twilight* phenomenon, it may seem that the film has been hyped to oblivion and only achieved mass popularity after filming was completed, but Robert noticed a trend early on. 'I don't really think even the production company knew how big it was going to become,' he considered. 'It's interesting, but as we were shooting it sort of got bigger and bigger and bigger, and more and more people started turning up to the set every day. By the end there were all these people coming out to the set who'd managed to find out where it was, which was a very strange experience.'

Though there were clues early on as to the popularity of *Twilight*, nothing could have prepared Robert Pattinson for what was to come.

Bella succumbs to Edward's otherworldly charms during Twilight's *prom scene finale.*

a twilight explosion

'When you're greeted by crowds of screaming fans it's like being in some medieval battle. I guess that's the closest analogy, especially after yesterday. A ton of people ran down the street outside the Apple Store. I felt like I was literally being charged by Celts.'
– Robert Pattinson

Twilight was originally scheduled to be released in the US on 12 December, 2008, but after the release of the new *Harry Potter* movie, *Harry Potter And The Half-Blood Prince*, was pushed back to July 2009, Summit Entertainment decided to pounce and push *Twilight* onto theatre screens as soon as possible. It subsequently received its US release on 21 November, competing with the Disney film *Bolt*, but little else that would detract from its viewing figures.

On its opening day *Twilight* earned a staggering $35.7 million, enough to almost recoup the entire cost of making the movie. It was the fourteenth best first-day haul in cinema history and Catherine Hardwicke became the only female director to enjoy an initial film gross that high. On the second day *Twilight* made the same figure again. The projections for possible profit beyond the first weekend verged on the astronomical.

The critical reaction, however, was somewhat lukewarm. Many fans were underwhelmed with the adaptation, and those who were new to *The Twilight Saga* may have struggled to understand certain elements at play in the film.

Overall, the reviews were mixed and often gave the film an average critique. The *Hollywood Reporter* called the movie 'An underwhelming vampire romance long on camp but short on emotional insight.' Yet they clearly viewed Robert Pattinson as the main success of *Twilight*, gushing, 'Pattinson, his eyes encased in dark contact lenses, skin pasty and hair swept back like a 1950s rocker, is the modern expression of vampirism. He's super strong yet delicate and like Stewart he is undeniably sexy.'

Entertainment Weekly went one step further, comparing Pattinson's character to bygone heroes of the literary and movie worlds. 'Edward is Romeo, Heathcliff, James Dean, and Brad Pitt all rolled into one,' the review panted, 'a scruffy, gorgeous bloodsucker pin-up who is really an angelic protector.'

Certain magazines were more critical in their views of Pattinson. *Empire* thought

Robert and Kristen on the red carpet at the Twilight
world premiere in Los Angeles, November 2008.

'Pattinson struggles at times – it's a demanding first lead role, requiring him to project a perennial restrained desire. He settles down eventually, but not before he's treated us to a series of hard-faced pouts.'

Some websites and magazines were distinctly unimpressed with the big screen adaptation. The *Austin Chronicle* acknowledged that 'Bella and Edward's courtship is played out with plenty of dreamy, slo-mo nuance', but jibed that 'Pattinson's cheekbones keep getting in the way of the story'.

Despite the occasional critical comments and cries of 'average', *Twilight* continued to be a dominant topic of media conversation, both in America and the UK. Its impact was so dramatic, in fact, that talk almost immediately began revolving around the sequels. Catherine Hardwicke admitted *Twilight* would have to do some 'major business' in order to continue, but by the end of November Robert Pattinson had reportedly been offered $12 million to appear in the second film adaptation of the *Twilight* series, *New Moon*.

Luckily for Pattinson, he was happy to continue to play Edward, especially as *New Moon* was his favourite book from the series, although as he would acknowledge, 'Edward is hardly in it.' Even during his performance for the first movie, however, Robert was thinking long-term, confirming that he 'tried to set up a performance which would last the three movies without me getting bored of it. Edward becomes such a different character in the later stories, and I love that, and tried to allude to that in the performance in this one.'

**'When something or someone is hyped and you're put at the forefront of a lot of things, people want to tear you down. That's kind of scary.'
– Robert Pattinson**

Over-thinking as usual, Robert further illuminated just why he couldn't wait to sink his teeth into his next Cullen role. 'I think you can really change the character at the end,' he mused. 'He's distraught and every ounce of confidence he has in the first one is gone by the end of the second one, by his reappearance at the end when he's essentially committing suicide. He can really completely change his image, like, nothing in the rest of the books. I can create something quite special with it, I think… if they let me.'

For Robert the plaudits and fan interest were increasing by the day. Shortly after he completed filming on the movie he revealed he had been 'completely and utterly ignorant until the last day of shooting of what *Twilight* really was. Even the budget didn't reflect that kind of phenomenon that it is now. It wasn't that kind of $200 million budget movie. It was a relatively low-budget thing. So I literally had no idea it would get this kind of attention.'

This 'kind of attention' referred to a global press tour, hundreds of interviews per week, TV appearances, the emergence of endless fan websites, and a general sense that Robert Pattinson was going to be a very popular actor for a long time to come.

Robert was used to the fan adulation by the time of *Twilight*'s release. But even after several months of personal appearances and continual adoration he couldn't quite understand the unique fan interest in either Edward Cullen or, indeed, Robert Pattinson.

Robert signs autographs for salivating fans before Twilight's *screening at the Rome International Film Festival, October 2008.*

At the Comic-Con convention in San Diego in July 2008 he had been exposed to the true nature of the devotion his role as Edward provoked. But was unprepared for the fan reaction, even as the time of his appearance neared. 'Until the moment I walked on stage, I had no idea,' he said bashfully, 'then they put the word "Twilight" on the screen and seven thousand girls were screaming for forty-five minutes.'

From there on in, everywhere Robert went there were screaming girls; he said he felt like one of the Beatles. Several appearances at various venues throughout the US had to be cancelled because the sheer amount of fans who had gathered was proving dangerous. Fan hysteria was rife at the NYC Apple Store where Robert had been due to make a 'meet and greet' appearance, and the event was cancelled. The same thing happened in San Francisco. The police were called in when three thousand young fans whipped themselves into an uncontrollable frenzy.

One of Robert's co-stars in *Twilight*, Peter Facinelli, told the *Los Angeles Times* of his concerns for Pattinson. 'I feel for Robert,' he said with regard to the legions of *Twilight*

Hell for leather: Kristen and Robert arrive at NBC Studios in New York to film an appearance on the Today *show, November 2008.*

'I've been involved in *Twilight* all year now.
I've been doing press for several weeks so I haven't really had time to reflect on what my life actually is.'
– Robert Pattinson

devotees. 'He didn't sign up for this knowing what it would become. The fan base has grown even since when we filmed it. There were underground fans when we started. I remember we'd all go to their websites and they all said, "All these actors are wrong for the roles. Facinelli doesn't have blonde hair – what are they thinking?" For Rob, he just signed up thinking it'd be a cool little movie. All of a sudden he's like the James Dean of

Voulez-vous coucher avec moi?
Robert promotes Twilight *in Paris, November 2008*

Left: *Robert's handprints are immortalised in cement at New York's Planet Hollywood, November 2008.*
Right: *Robert appears on* The Tonight Show With Jay Leno *in Los Angeles, November 2008.*

today. That's a lot [to] put on a guy's shoulders, but hopefully he'll be okay. He's kind of nerve-wracked. He doesn't like to leave his apartment a lot. But I think it'll be good. This will bring good things to him.'

Money, fame and fan-worship were not exactly primary motivations for Robert Pattinson – in fact, none of it really mattered to him. Therefore, quite understandably, he had trouble coping with the spotlight and the reverence afforded him, especially when the initial reactions had been so brutal. 'I don't know why it still shocks me,' he reflected. 'I mean, I've been going for the last three weeks, just going to different cities all around the world, just to get to these planned mobbings, where everybody just screams and screams and screams. But every single time, I get so nervous, and kind of cold sweats, and everything. So I doubt that I am ready.'

Robert's travels to promote the movie also took him to European destinations. It was at one particular appearance in Italy that the actor inexplicably broke down. 'I started crying in Italy,' he confided to one interviewer. 'Like, completely involuntarily. It was really embarrassing. I didn't even know I was. Kristen, I think, turned around to me. And she's like, "Are you crying?" When you're in a situation that feels like it's gotten out of control, I find that the more you stress out about it, the worse it would get.'

One may have suspected that Robert did not worry what his fans thought, nor ventured too deeply into his fan mail, but in actual fact it was something he took time to regularly look through. His mail was sent over from his London post box, and it often consisted of personal presents as well as fawning letters. 'I go through tons and tons of it at a time,' Robert said. 'I get sent some good stuff. I've gotten some really good books. I

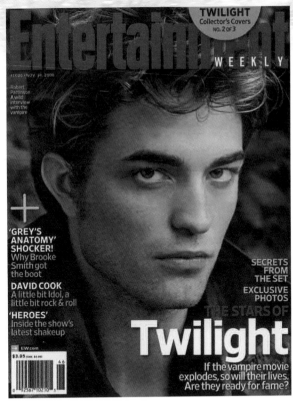

In the run-up to Twilight's *November 2008 release, Robert was featured on two* Entertainment Weekly *front covers*

had this amazing thing made by a fan website, this really amazing bound book with all of these notes inside it. I mean, it must have taken ages to make. I remember thinking, "Why?" But, no, it was amazing. Someone sent me a book I'm reading right now, a book of Charles Baudelaire poems. I thought, "Wow, I was going to buy that." That was nice.'

In fact, in Robert's wary opinion his correspondence was *too* nice. Everything was positive and it didn't quite tally with his opinion of potential crazed stalkers. He presumed someone somewhere was weeding out any psychotic letters or presents before he received them. 'I go

'I'm not really in the right job. I don't like having my photo taken. I don't like the attention.'
– Robert Pattinson

through it myself, but I think I might get them censored,' he reasoned, 'because I'm always expecting to get the one thing that says, "I know where you live and I'm going to kill you!" I'm always expecting that to come, but it never seems to arrive. I never get any negative letters.'

Letters were one thing, but during his personal appearances Robert often came across unusual reactions and – in one particular case – an extremely young fan with a bizarre request. Pattinson told *E! Online* that a seven-year-old girl had asked him to bite her. 'It wasn't a joke,' he said. 'I looked at her and thought, "Do you know what you're saying?"' Needless to say, Robert turned down the request with his usual good grace.

It is, however, hard to know just how to deal with certain requests. There was an incident where, as Robert described, 'A mother recently gave me her baby and asked, "Can you please bite his head?"' Robert also revealed that he receives 'letters that say,

Teen

stars real lives

50
HOLLYWOOD HOTTIES
start crushing now

NO GUY?
NO BIGGIE!
7 reasons it's cool to be single

TWILIGHT TAKEOVER
cast secrets revealed!

AMAZING HAIR
get it all winter
(see p. 82)

SO YOU HATE HER
but could you ever be friends?

seventeen

teenmag.com

Winter 2008 $3.00

0 74820 08658 2 3 8>

Ent...men
WEEKL

#1024 • DECEMBER 5, 200

YO COMPLE GUI
TWILIGHT EXPLODES

»The Monster Opening Week
»Inside Scoop on the Se
»What's Next for the and Robert Pattir

+

MERYL STREEP
The Legendary Actress on Life as a Box Office Titan

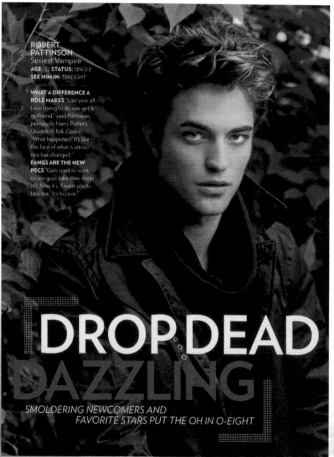

ROBERT PATTINSON
Sexiest Vampire
AGE: 22 **STATUS:** SINGLE
SEE HIM IN: *TWILIGHT*

WHAT A DIFFERENCE A ROLE MAKES "Last year all I was trying to do was get a girlfriend," says Pattinson, previously Harry Potter's Quidditch foil, Cedric. "What happened? It's like the face of what is attractive has changed."
FANGS ARE THE NEW PECS "Girls used to want to see guys take their shirts off. Now it's, 'I want you to bite me.' It's bizarre."

DROP DEAD
DAZZLING

SMOLDERING NEWCOMERS AND FAVORITE STARS PUT THE OH IN O-EIGHT

TO
die
FOR

The *Twilight* novels have enraptured a generation of girls—and their moms. This month, the movie arrives. Here's a wild interview with the vampire, a candid talk with his mortal love— and the inside story of bringing the phenom to the screen.

PHOTOGRAPHS BY JAMES WHITE

VAMPIRE HUNKS

THE SEDUCTIVE BLOODSUCKERS OF *TWILIGHT* **HAVE FEMALE HEARTS RACING!**

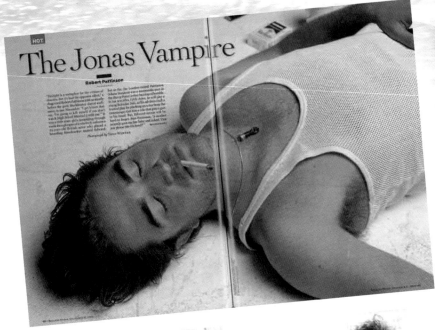

The Jonas Vampire

Robert Pattinson

Photograph by Tesh Wigdor

"All the News That Fits"

The Vampire Heartthrob

HOT ACTOR The hottest fangs in Hollywood undeniably belong to Robert Pattinson, the wild-haired, 22-year-old British actor whose turn as a brooding vampire in the goth blockbuster *Twilight* is now causing hormonal pandemonium in movie theaters across America. "Eight-year-old girls say, 'Can you bite me?'" Pattinson says. "It's like, 'Do you even know what that means?'" Pattinson will next go on to impress older audiences by playing another hirsute extrovert: Salvador Dali..*60*

The Twilight Zone

For all Buffy's efforts, vampires have been sinking their teeth ever deeper into Generation W's pop culture. To a spate of hugely profitable books and HBO's *True Blood*, add this month's *Twilight*, a movie based on Stephenie Meyer's blockbuster saga, which has sold millions of copies in the U.S. alone. As starlet Kristen Stewart plays the mortal innocent to Robert Pattinson's undead rebel, JAMES WOLCOTT explores the buried messages of this bloodsucking invasion

VAMP IT UP
Stars of the movie adaptation of "The Twilight Saga": Cam Gigandet as James, Kristen Stewart as Bella, and Robert Pattinson as Edward, photographed in Los Angeles.

THE VAMPIRE
Robert Pattinson
BY KAREN VALBY

Less than a year ago, Robert Pattinson, a British actor known only for a small part in *Harry Potter and the Goblet of Fire*, was picked to play Edward, the brooding, beautiful vampire at the center of Stephenie Meyer's best-selling *Twilight* saga. Fans revolted immediately. They were furious over the surprise casting of a relative unknown who failed to live up to their idea of the immaculate demigod drawn from their book's own vivid pages. By the time Pattinson's mother told him she'd read online that her only son was wretched and ugly and had the face of a gargoyle, the author found herself awash in guilt. "I apologized to Rob," says Meyer "for ruining his life."

Her teenage girls have their usual swings. It wasn't long before the *Twilight* universe—17 million-word-wide readers addicted to the tortured romance between Edward and a mortal schoolgirl named Bella—embraced the 22-year-old

CoverStory

Inside the Twilight romance!

Robert Pattinson and Kristen Stewart play young lovers in their new movie — and their chemistry didn't stop offscreen

With advance tickets selling out and millions of fans craving wait-ins at public-eye appearances, the vampire drama *Twilight* is shaping up to be one of the biggest blockbusters of the year. But the real reason the movie — based on Stephenie Meyer's best-selling book — looks like such a success in the cinema romance chemistry between costars Kristen Stewart and Robert Pattinson. Kristen, 18, plays Bella Swan, a mortal teenage girl who falls for handsome vampire Edward Cullen, played by Robert, 22. "Kristen and Rob bonded from the moment they met," says an insider. "They get along so well people most convinced they were secretly in love."

Instant connection
Were they? Sparks certainly flew from the start. After Kristen performed a pivotal love scene with the four leading contenders for the role of Edward, *Twilight's* director, Catherine Hardwicke, was still unsure about whom to

cast. Not Kristen. "I was like, 'Are you joking? I can't do the movie unless Rob does it,'" she says. "Rob and I could see each other [in the role]. I basically cast Rob."

And the feeling was mutual for the British hunk. "When I got into the room with Kristen, there was just a certain chemistry," he says. "She's basically the reason I did the movie."

Bonding time
Located in Portland, Ore., during filming, Robert and Kristen only grew

Why everyone's talking about Twilight

IT'S A HOT READ The romance novels (Twilight, New Moon, Eclipse and Breaking Dawn) has sold a whopping 17 million copies. All four books are among Amazon.com's top 20 best sellers.

IT'S EVERYWHERE The romance has been selling licensed merchandise.

THERE'S VAMPIRE MANIA Move over, Buffy, there's a new mob of undead in town. Besides *Twilight*, which has already sold out hundreds of showings nationwide, *True Blood* is a major hit for HBO.

"I think he's really handsome."
—Kristen Stewart on costar Robert Pattinson

"'I'm going to kill myself if you don't watch *High School Musical 2* with me.'"

These were some of the more bizarre demands he received, but more worrying for Pattinson was the possibility of seriously obsessive or crazed fans. 'My brain doesn't really accept fame,' he explained, 'so it's fine. I can be put anywhere and it just goes completely over my head. I just don't want to get shot or stabbed. I don't want someone to have a needle and I'll get AIDS afterwards. That's my only real fear. Whenever I see a crowd I always think that. It's like being on a plane. I think the bottom is going to hit the runway when it's taking off.'

Part of Robert's paranoia stemmed from the fact he knew the *Twilight* series was open to anyone, but seemed to invite extremists. The incident with the seven-year-old girl asking for a bite did not help assuage his fears. 'I think that for a lot of the fans of the book it's become a kind of cult now that they like defending,' Robert observed. 'Other young people want to join it because they feel like they're missing out on something. I think it's a rolling stone gathering more and more people with it. I don't know for sure. I can't really tell you. What I always thought about it when I read the book was that it seemed like Stephenie Meyer completely believed that she was Bella, and so in a lot of ways, when you're reading it, it

**'Now the film's out I can't walk down the street without being pounced on.'
– Robert Pattinson**

seems uncomfortably voyeuristic, like you're reading somebody's fantasy. And after meeting Stephenie Meyer, it's absolutely not the case. But I really, really thought when I was going to meet Stephenie that it was going to be a very strange experience, with her thinking that I was a character. I think that's one of the reasons, that it's just such an intimate thing that people can really belong to. It's just one of these rare things that everybody wants to have a piece of.'

Such obsession even extended to the state of Robert's hair. As many websites were running out of Pattinson-related trivia and news they saw fit to concentrate on his famously unruly tangle of locks, which, according to Robert, was plagued with dandruff (perhaps as a consequence of his leaving it unwashed for weeks on end). He told *Entertainment Tonight* he was 'very aware' of his dandruff. 'Well, there's many, many flaws,' he explained. 'Earlier on, I didn't know what was going on, I was like going nuts. I was supposed to have a little nap this afternoon; I just shook my hair all afternoon to see how much dandruff could possibly come out of my hair. It was intense.'

In just a matter of months Robert Pattinson had progressed from a potential up-and-coming star who few people could imagine as Edward Cullen to a recognised talent who inspired as many column inches for the state of his hair as his onscreen performances. It is arguable that few people would have known much about him just six months previously, yet by November 2008 he was appearing on vaunted celebrity TV programmes such as *The Ellen DeGeneres Show* and *The Tyra Banks Show*.

What Robert was absolutely certain of, however, is his plan if the worst is to happen and his popularity suddenly wanes. 'My attitude from the beginning has been, "If you start failing, do not start going on reality TV shows."'

Eye of the media storm: Robert and Kristen attend the Twilight *premiere in Munich, December 2008.*

fame and
the future

'All my life I've hated crowds.
Now I only have to step outdoors and I'm at the centre of one.
It's very cool but it's very uncomfortable too.'
– Robert Pattinson

Robert Pattinson was always a keen musician and music fan, having played the piano from a very early age, and – as he grew older – embraced influences that ran the gamut from blues to alternative rock.

'I have been playing the piano for my entire life – since I was three or four,' he said. 'And the guitar – I used to play classical guitar from when I was about five to twelve years of age. Then I didn't play guitar for years. About four or five years ago, I got out the guitar again and just started playing blues and stuff. I am not very good at the guitar, but I am alright.'

Robert played well enough to join a band, though his involvement would eventually be put to one side due to his other commitments. He described the origins of a band he was once part of: 'Bad Girls belonged to my first girlfriend's current boyfriend and he was having an open mic night. He invited me to sing, but it was just a bit of fun. We only played a couple of gigs. It is just a couple of friends of mine and some other people that I had met fairly recently. We just wanted to start a band for something to do. A lot of my friends are actors and we have so little to do all the time, so instead of just being bored, we were like, "Why not start a band?" So we did. I had kind of roll-on, roll-off musicians. I still try and play, but it's weird now since when I'm trying to do it as an actor, it always seems kind of cheesy. I liked playing at open mics in bars and stuff because it was the only time I really felt free. I did a couple of gigs in LA and people filmed [them] and put them on the internet. It just ruins the whole experience. You're like, "Oh, that wasn't the point." So I stopped. I'm going to wait for all this to die down before I start doing live gigs again.'

Robert also wrote his own music for pleasure, drawing inspiration from the solo style of his two favourite artists. He describes his material as 'Van Morrison-ish, Jeff Buckley-ish stuff,' admitting: 'I don't know much about contemporary music. I do have an iPod but I listen to a lot of old blues. I listen to John Lee Hooker and Elmore James. I have been listening to them for years.'

*'I was at a photo shoot the other day, and people were saying,
"They say we can't touch your hair. You have trademarked hair!" No, I don't.'*

Other favourites on his portable music player include the likes of Kings of Leon, James Brown, Curtis Mayfield and Neil Young. There is also Robert's friend and musician Johnny Flynn, who plays a country, rock and folk hybrid. 'I grew up with some amazing musicians in London who are still my friends,' said Robert. 'Marcus Foster, Bobby Long and Sam Bradley are recording their albums now, but Johnny Flynn completed his one a while ago. I just saw him play in LA and he was incredible. But he's always been incredible so I can't say I was surprised. The album is great; no one else does music like him at all.'

Pattinson spoke with reverence of the veteran Van Morrison (whose every album he owns). 'I saw Van Morrison last night at the Hollywood Bowl. I've seen him five times before and he really pulled it out of the bag. He played like it was thirty years ago. I would love to do something with him now. He was my inspiration for doing music in the first place. Yes, he's still got it. The whole thing was unbelievable. He was just as free as he was when he was younger, which was amazing. He has such a visionary and unique take on what structure in songwriting is, what singing is, and what can be achieved emotionally and spiritually through music.'

> 'It's definitely changed my career a lot. People take me more seriously, I guess, in the industry.'
> – Robert Pattinson

Many people who have heard Robert Pattinson sing have compared his soulful, wavering voice to that of his other musical hero, Jeff Buckley. Fans have even suggested that Robert would be perfect to play the musician in a film based on his short life (Buckley drowned in 1997, aged thirty). According to online news reports, Pattinson himself is keen to portray Buckley in the frequently discussed but as yet unproduced biopic.

The soundtrack for *Twilight* would become big business, released in two formats. One featured the original score for the movie and the other was a compilation of the various artists whose songs were included in the film – Muse, Linkin Park and Paramore among them. Robert would find himself included on the second CD, though it was completely by accident.

'I did a scene where I played a thing that I made up,' he remembered. 'It was the best piano piece I've ever done in my life but it didn't really fit... The song on the soundtrack, "Never Think" – my best friend who taught me how to play the guitar wrote the lyrics for it last year, and I made it into a song, and the other one ["Let Me Sign"] me and another guy wrote. They weren't meant for the movie, but Catherine heard them and put them in the cut, and I didn't know they would be on the soundtrack. I had thought it would be quite cool to have it be a secret thing and not have my name in the credits. Like a marketing gimmick. It was nice, and also helped my friends as well.'

Unfortunately for Robert, ever the rebel, his name would be included in the credits, and was in fact a major selling point for the soundtrack. It was thanks to Nikki Reed, who plays Rosalie Hale in the *Twilight* movies, that Robert's original songs ended up on the soundtrack CD. 'I think Nikki gave a CD of stuff I had recorded on my computer to Catherine Hardwicke, and I recorded it years ago,' Robert clarified. 'I think Catherine just put it into a cut and then said, "Look at this," and she played it and it kind of worked. I hadn't even realised what it was at first and it kind of fit really well.'

Robert tries to reclaim his anonymity at Los Angeles International Airport, November 2008.

Catherine Hardwicke recalled the sequence of events that resulted in Robert appearing on the soundtrack: 'Nikki Reed and Kristen would tell me, "Robert, he's got a good voice. It's really intense, it's really interesting." So I'd see Rob in the morning and go, "Hey Rob, I really wanna hear you sing." He'd say, "Oh no, it's not ready, it's not good and no one can hear it," really just protesting everyday. He was so shy about it…' Eventually, of course, the good-willed intervention of Nikki Reed ensured him a place on the soundtrack, though he would still have issues with his name appearing in the credits.

> 'I'm not really interested in having a music career. I don't care if people buy my stuff or not.'
> – Robert Pattinson

Robert revealed that in the build-up to the filming of *Twilight*, he relied on certain kinds of music to colour his mood. 'I was listening to a lot of girl acoustics, like some depressing stuff,' he said. 'Some Alela Diane – who actually lived in Portland – a composer called Georgy Ligeti, who I thought was kind of relevant. It was kind of the opposite of what Stephenie was listening to. She has very hard, almost punk stuff, and I listened to really depressing acoustic stuff.'

As a compromise in announcing his identity on the liner notes, Robert is credited as 'Rob Pattinson' – though he could easily have gone under his nicknames RPattz or Spunk

Ransom. In fact, Robert explained he had a dislike of his birth name and preferred the nicknames. 'I hate my name or any reference to my name,' he said morosely. Elaborating on the origin of his nicknames, Robert explained: 'RPattz. I guess it kind of makes sense. It's my initial, and a bit of my name. I don't know. At least it's not an insult. It sounds kind of like antacid or something. Spunk. There's a girl that's called Ransom. I'd like to be called "Ransom Spunk", or "Spunk Ransom".'

Pattinson's songs are without doubt two of the strongest additions to the soundtrack album. 'Never Think' possesses a lovelorn melody, featuring Pattinson and a bare acoustic guitar. The track is reminiscent of a slew of American alternative performers, most notably Pearl Jam and, of course, Jeff Buckley, but more obscurely, Pattinson's wavering voice brings to mind the Seattle-based songwriter Shawn Smith. Though he barely rises above a whisper, his vocal performance is deeply affecting. The lyrics pertain perfectly to Edward and Bella. 'Girl save your soul,' Pattinson croons. 'Before it's too far gone and before nothing can be done. Without me you got it all so hold on.'

> 'Music is a big part of my life – not enormous. I go through phases, especially when I'm in London, where all I do is play music.'
> – Robert Pattinson

On 'Let Me Sign' Pattinson's voice is more audibly Van Morrison-indebted. This song is shorter, yet full of potential, and deserves more room to breathe than its two-minute length allows. Ultimately and most importantly, however, it is integrity and grittiness that Robert brings to his performances, and it is abundantly clear that he makes music for his own pleasure and catharsis. As Catherine Hardwicke observed, 'One of my favourite parts of making the movie was watching Rob play the music he wrote. He just lets it out, and it breaks your heart.'

As Robert was rapidly becoming a big star, it naturally brought attention to his inclusion on the soundtrack, which – perhaps as a consequence – sold extraordinarily well, shifting media and fan focus onto his musical abilities. Something he was not entirely comfortable with.

Within its first week of release the *Twilight* compilation sold 165,000 copies – some of the best ever initial sales figures for a soundtrack. It eventually became Atlantic Records' best-selling soundtrack of all time, and its success gave Catherine Hardwicke cause for reflection. After all, she had – against Robert's better instincts – persuaded him to include his material in the movie. 'Now I feel guilty,' she said.

'I didn't really think about it beforehand,' Robert confirmed. 'I didn't know it was going to be on the soundtrack or anything. I wanted to do it under another name because I thought it would be distracting, which it has been. So it's probably all been a big mistake, but I like the idea of it and I just think the song fits and I did not think it sounded like me. So I thought it would just work, but I don't know. I'm not trying to get a music career out of it or anything.'

Robert admitted he would like to make an album of his own material, but that it would

Robert faces another day in front of the camera at a Twilight *press conference. This time in Los Angeles at the Beverly Wilshire Hotel, November 2008.*

most likely be released under a pseudonym. With typical humility he explained, 'I might make an album, but not through a record company or anything. I'd like to do something independent. I'd just like to have it just for myself so I can work with good musicians and stuff.' He has since quipped: 'Maybe I could just do it under "Edward Cullen" and see what happens.'

It is often said that every actor is a frustrated musician and vice versa. In Robert's case, however, he can ably combine the two. Music is in his soul, and given that he does not care for album sales, he can create and take solace in songs any time he wishes. 'I wouldn't do it at the same time as acting,' he confessed. 'I mean, the whole thing I find quite embarrassing. I don't like the idea of saying, "You're in the public eye, now is the time to release an album because people will buy it." I don't care if people buy it or not.'

When his musical ability was brought into question after a special performance in Los Angeles, Robert was able to confirm those sentiments ever more deeply. He played an unannounced, one-off acoustic set under the name 'Bobby Dupea' at the famous Whisky-A-Go-Go club, but was unexpectedly filmed. The clip of his performance was broadcast online and many felt entitled to criticise his act. 'I was so not ready for the scrutiny,' Robert complained. 'I haven't touched a guitar since. When you know you have to be good every time, you never want to do it again.' Tellingly, Bobby Dupea was

> 'I feel like I have nothing to talk about to my friends anymore. It's going to really destroy me when I go back home.'
> – Robert Pattinson

the name of Jack Nicholson's character in the 1970 film *Five Easy Pieces*, in which he played a pianist. It was also rumoured that Robert used this alias to post his own songs online on a MySpace page, long before they were included on the *Twilight* soundtrack.

Pattinson certainly does not need the additional money or fame, and it is no wonder he already has a sour impression of the music business. He is well aware of how the industry functions after seeing his sister work hard for many years. 'I don't think people should look for a record contract,' he explained. 'My sister works so hard to make money and I think it ruins you, I think it's a lot easier to make money in the acting world, not that it's easier, but there aren't so many pressures on you. You don't have to be so humble, where in the music industry you have to really bow down to a lot of people to get noticed.'

Dealing with fame was always going to be the hardest part of a successful career for Robert Pattinson. Given his phenomenal looks and gentlemanly charms, it was inevitable that he would be inundated with female interest, and the consequences of this were both positive and negative.

News of Robert's love life was apparently most appealing to fans. Only a year before his success in *Twilight*, he claimed he had struggled to find female companionship, revealing, 'When I was in London, it was like, I couldn't get a date at all. I don't know why. That's all I talked about the whole of last year, that I need to get a girlfriend. And then this year, I could have any twelve-year-old I wanted.' Robert actually commanded the affections of a far wider age-range, as Catherine Hardwicke had personally experienced. She recalled one

Robert arches an eyebrow during a Twilight *photocall at the Hotel de Crillon in Paris, December 2008.*

Robert and his old friend Tom Sturridge greet the paparazzi after a night of drinking at the Chateau Marmont in Los Angeles, November 2008.

particularly revealing incident: 'When I brought my seventy-year-old mother to the set I asked her if she'd like to meet Rob and Kristen. To which mum promptly replied: "Just Rob."'

Pattinson hit headlines in gossip treasure trove the *National Enquirer*, as well as countless other showbiz websites. Sometimes his quotes were a little contradictory. In early November 2008 he said, 'I'm not dating anyone. I mean, I theoretically don't avoid it. But it's weird. I've been going to the same places every time I go to LA, because they're the only places I know. And now everybody kind of knows me in those places. So it's like – I don't know. Just knowing that people will talk about stuff, and – you know. It's very uncomfortable. And also, if you try and chat people up, everyone's like, "Oh, he's such a – you're just an actor. You probably go around sleeping with everybody." So it kind of has the reverse effect of what you would have thought.'

Various tabloid rumour-mills have linked Pattinson with several women in the public eye, including Brazilian model Annelyse Schoenberger and twenty-two-year-old American actress Camilla Belle. Robert has been characteristically unperturbed by these media stories, however, and refuted all suggestions that he was currently attached. 'I am single at the moment, but I read stories in the magazines and papers that I am dating so and so,' he sighed. 'But it's not true. But they are very good guesses because I always fancy the girl they pair me up with. I'm hoping it's the girl herself who has made it up – then I'm in with a real chance. Maybe I should start getting in contact with them!'

He added: 'The stuff I find attractive in women, I always regret finding attractive. I always

'In England if you want to look rough, you go out and get really drunk and come in looking really hungover, but if you do that in America, it's like, "Have you got a drinking problem?"'
– Robert Pattinson

like a kind of madness in a woman, and when they are really, really strong. And they're the worst – mental, strong women!'

Some felt Robert may have been holding out for Kristen Stewart, especially as he had described her as being particularly strong. The interest may be mutual, as Stewart often compliments her new friend. In one interview she stated, 'Oh, he's like a little tortured artist. He's British. He's tall. He always looks like he's thinking about something. And he's quite witty. So he's pretty sexy.'

But Robert is nonplussed about any public reaction he might encounter. 'I like not really caring what people think of me. I mean, I kinda do, but at the same I don't

'Once you're becoming the "hot thing" or whatever, magazines say "Oh we want to do a feature" and I've just started to say "No", because as soon as you start putting yourself out there – people want to tear you down. And I don't want to tempt anybody to want to tear me down.'
– Robert Pattinson

at all. I can't really tell which one is true. I feel the same in my head as before I guess. I was quite a paranoid person anyway, so it doesn't really feed well when people are looking at you. I'm not really in the right job. I don't like having my photo taken. I don't like the attention.'

As 2008 came to a close and his name became evermore droppable in Hollywood circles, Robert Pattinson struggled to contend with the sudden paparazzi attention his appearance could stir. 'I think someone follows me,' he said of the demonised snappers. 'They do the most random stuff. I get a photo taken through a burger drive-through window and it's like, "What?" They always seem like they're six feet away. I don't understand. I'm walking around and I don't see anybody.'

Several celebrity-fixated publications, including the *National Enquirer*, were quick to draw attention to Robert's supposedly hard-partying ways, reporting that on numerous occasions he had been seen knocking back cocktails in various LA hotspots – the notorious Chateau Marmont among them – and was supposedly on his way to developing a serious alcohol problem.

Robert responded to these accusations with characteristic nonchalance. 'It's a very different culture,' he said of America. 'There really isn't a pub scene in LA, and people here don't understand how it's such a normal thing to drink in pubs in London. They think it's very strange and there's such a stigma attached to it here, but it just seems normal to me. In England if you want to look rough, you go out and get really drunk and come in looking really hungover, but if you do that in America, it's like, "Have you got a drinking problem?"'

It was no wonder Robert was so laidback; he had, some months earlier, predicted the media reaction to his regular forays into club land. 'I keep getting photographed coming out of these lame clubs. It's so embarrassing. There was a week where every single night I was going out and getting photographed by the paparazzi or TMZ and I realised, "Oh, my God, I look like a complete alcoholic!"'

'Sudden fame is kind of… I'm not really sure how to deal with it yet.' – Robert Pattinson

It was clear that Robert was attempting to remain as normal as possible, albeit in an extraordinary situation, one that his family viewed as a fantastic fairytale. He seemed perplexed at the changes taking place in his life after finding fame on a huge scale, though he would try to downplay its impact. 'At the moment it hasn't changed my life a huge amount,' he said. 'I'm just going from place to place. It's so new to me I can't really be jaded. It's not really going to my head because I don't even know what it is. It's strange how you get treated differently by people in a very brief amount of time. When you ask someone to go out to dinner they're like, "Do you want me to?" It's like, "What are you talking about, why would I have asked you?" Funny little things like that happen.'

Ultimately, for Robert there was only one female worth mentioning: 'My dog is the only lady friend in my life. I have a really girly dog but she hasn't got a girly attitude. My dog is a little bit like Beyoncé – it has a Beyoncé walk, which is strange for a little terrier.'

Of course, the hottest rumours were about which role Robert Pattinson would tackle next. Unlike many of his peers he wasn't about to sign up for three or four other movies straight away, instead spending time promoting *Twilight* and looking forward to a break from all the media interest. Nevertheless, there were a number of parts for which he was already being considered, and he was regularly checking out new scripts.

Robert also revealed that he would like 'to be in a Terry Gilliam film, playing a midget. I'd like to do a Godard film, or one with Michael Cimino. But the script means more to me than the people involved.'

With filmmaking integrity in mind, Robert revealed that in 2009 he would be starring alongside Dennis Hopper and Rosario Dawson in a movie called *Parts Per Billion*. 'I don't want to curse them, but I am doing this thing called *Parts Per Billion*,' he confirmed, 'which is a kind of existential love story set against the end of the world. It stars three couples, three different generations. It's in LA. I have no idea how to explain it. It's one of the most lyrical scripts that I have ever read in my life. I've never seen a script like this. It's a kind of treatise in marriage. How your future can be based on a relationship with someone at different time periods. It's very strange. I am quite looking forward to doing it. It's very different.'

Unfortunately, and despite his enthusiasm for the script, Robert's commitment to *New Moon*, the second film of the *Twilight* franchise, meant he had to withdraw from *Parts Per Billion*. On 8 January 2009, Robert's manager Nicholas Frenkel confirmed to MTV News that 'the prep time and production schedule on *New Moon* haven't left enough time for Robert to work on *Parts Per Billion* in the first quarter of this year'.

Robert's ambitions, however, are not limited to acting, and he has already set his sights on a new goal – seeking to gain a hand in how the film industry is controlled. 'I want to have a production company by the time I'm twenty-six,' he revealed. 'I guess I'm just a control freak. I don't like the way the film industry is. If you come with a good script and then it goes to the studios and gets financing, it all gets changed because they want to make money. And it's like, how do you know if it's going to make money or not? All you're doing is making it generic when you do that, and making it generic is no guarantee that it's going to make money either. The only way to abandon that is to take risks, and you need to be able to trust people. So you get a company together with people you know are good and, you know, work hard and you can make good stuff. That's kind of what I want to do.'

Robert would of course be filming *New Moon* in March 2009, though this time it would be without the presence of Catherine Hardwicke. The director's departure allegedly met with some resistance from both Robert and Kristen Stewart. It was reported that Hardwicke had been relieved of her duties for Summit Entertainment, and her successor was eventually named as Chris Weitz, who had previously directed fantasy epic *The Golden Compass*. The *Chicago Sun-Times* revealed that a source had confirmed that both Robert and Kristen 'are both very upset' over Hardwicke's release. The source continued, 'They are committed to doing at least the next *Twilight* film and probably the one after that, but they really wanted to do them with Catherine.' It was divulged that Stewart had told a close associate of the second movie, 'I sure hope they don't fuck it up.'

'If I'm getting paid $12 million a movie I'd walk around naked. That's all nonsense. I don't know who makes that stuff up.'
– Robert Pattinson

At least the chance of a movie role unrelated to *Twilight* gave Robert a break from his incessant promotion of Edward Cullen. 'I feel as if I've been in this *Twilight* bubble where I never see the outside world,' he said. 'I get a lot of people saying, "How does it feel to be an overnight sensation?" But I literally have not been to a restaurant in such a long time. I have no idea what my real life is like any more. Maybe when the film comes out and I go back to London, I can actually see what the real difference is.'

Robert did return to London to promote *Twilight*, and instantly realised that his fan base stretched far beyond America – in fact he was just as popular in his home city, a fact that amazed him. On 3 December, Robert and Kristen Stewart appeared at the *Twilight* movie premiere in London's Leicester Square. The pair walked a suitably black carpet, which was blasted with dry ice for vampiric effect. They were met by thousands of screaming fans who, it has to be said, were mainly female and there to see Robert Pattinson. On his whirlwind tour Robert squeezed in a number of interviews on all the major UK channels. When talking to GMTV he spoke of the *Twilight* phenomenon. 'The extent to which I've seen the insanity around this story, I don't get it,' he shrugged. 'I read the book and the whole series and I can understand they're very addictive, but seeing the extent to which some people are just obsessed. I mean people yesterday at the premiere; some were like, "I've come from Brazil just to stand here for the premiere."'

During the interview Robert was pressed as to how this made him feel. He seemed perplexed and revealed: 'I used to get so stressed out because people are screaming at you. And you just think, "What do I have to do? I can't give anything back to you at all." Literally, I'm like, "Do you wanna come home with me?" Please don't answer that! I'm just saying it to be nice!'

> 'You get a bit of heat and everybody says you're this, you're that. Then it dies down.
> – Robert Pattinson

He told another interviewer about attending premieres, saying, 'When I go I guess I'm trying to promote it, but I'm not even promoting it. I'm just there to get screamed at. I don't even know what I'm supposed to be doing. It's a surreal experience. The only thing I've done all year was go around to cities and have people scream at me and stuff and ask things like, "What's it like to play the most beautiful person in the world?" I'm going to go back and start talking to my friends, being like, "Yeah, well this other person asked me how is it to play the most beautiful person in the world and then I went to this room and there's five thousand people screaming at me." I feel like I have nothing to talk about to my friends anymore. It's going to really destroy me when I go back home.'

By the end of 2008, Robert was in need of a rest. In late December he was spotted in Los Angeles with a new, closely-cropped haircut that seemed to symbolise his taking a break from all the *Twilight*-inspired hysteria of the previous year. He returned to London to spend Christmas with his family and friends, and was spotted drinking in some of his old haunts around the city. He even seemed to have rediscovered his love of playing live music, when he performed at an open mic night in Soho, reportedly silencing the room with a brilliant performance.

It will certainly take some time for Robert to return to reality. Perhaps he might never be able to re-establish his normal life. The actor himself remains in a state of disbelief about his worldwide fame, and with characteristic humility has revealed as much about Robert Pattinson as you could ever want to know. 'I've never been hugely popular or anything in my life, so it's going to be weird,' he said. 'I hope I get a bit of an ego afterwards.'

'I'm just going from place to place,' Robert said.
'It's so new to me I can't really be jaded.'

phenomenon

'Where can the hype go?'
– Robert Pattinson

Robert's Christmas and New Year return to London provided him with a well-earned recuperation period following the mania of the preceding months. 'I miss the smell of London,' he confessed. 'I almost cried because I missed it so much.' He spent several nights drinking at the capital's infamous celebrity hangout the Groucho Club with old friend and television presenter Miquita Oliver, his newly shorn hair hidden beneath a black winter hat. 'When people say something has become a trademark, you have got to get rid of it,' Robert said of his controversial decision to trim his famous tresses. 'It's the worst.'

Homesickness, it seemed, was likely to be a fixture in his life for the foreseeable future, and by mid-February it was time to return to Los Angeles for his first public appearance of 2009, at the Eighty-First Annual Academy Awards on 22 February. Robert and Kristen had been asked to co-present at the Oscars ceremony together, an offer that Stewart declined. (When her father, John Stewart, was asked the reason for this by *Access Hollywood*, he replied that his daughter would present at the Oscars, 'When it's a great movie, not just one that makes a lot of money' – a statement that was inevitably interpreted as a snub by many *Twilight* fans.) Robert, however, was thrilled by the request, revealing that he'd initially thought it was 'a joke': 'I still can't get over it,' he told an interviewer on the red carpet. 'I was just laughing in the car on the way here. It's completely ridiculous.' He also admitted that in rehearsals for the ceremony, he'd 'messed it up catastrophically, so I'm probably going to do that again and be the massive let-down of the entire show'.

Robert, who was sat in the second row of the auditorium amidst Hollywood royalty (positioned directly behind Best Actor nominee Mickey Rourke), presented a video montage of 'what love looked like in 2008' with *Mamma Mia!* actress Amanda Seyfried, in front of an estimated audience of one billion. 'I got there and I'm sitting in the second

'I still can't get over it,' Robert said of his attendance at the 2009 Oscars.
'I was laughing in the car on the way here. It's completely ridiculous.'

row. It was unbelievable. I keep thinking that something terrible is going to happen. "Death" is the only thing I'm thinking the whole time. I just used up all my luck so I'm probably going to die at twenty-three or something.'

Whilst attending a sequence of post-ceremony parties, he drank champagne and chatted with fellow teen pin-ups Zac Efron and Vanessa Hudgens, and was stunned to be approached by actress Robin Wright Penn, whose husband Sean Penn had just won the Best Actor Oscar for his role in *Milk*. 'I thought that was kind of amazing...' Robert said. 'It was very, very surreal.'

At an early-hours Oscars after party hosted by talent agent Patrick Whitesell in the Hollywood Hills, Robert was reported to have spent an hour in conversation with Paris Hilton before sharing a 'private' moment with the heiress in the garden. (After seeing *Twilight*, Hilton had publicly described Pattinson as 'a beautiful man and an amazing actor'.) At 4:30am, Robert departed to catch a flight to Tokyo for *Twilight*'s Japanese premiere on 27 February, where he would be reunited with co-stars Kristen Stewart and Taylor Lautner. The trio greeted the thrilled crowds of Japanese fans at Ebisu Garden Palace beneath a torrential downpour, and Pattinson later went to a karaoke bar near his hotel with Hugh Jackman, who was in Tokyo promoting Baz Luhrmann's outback epic *Australia*. Robert then flew directly from Tokyo to Vancouver, Canada to join rehearsals with the cast of *New Moon*, which was to commence its three-month shoot in early March.

'I'm not massively concerned about doing lots of acting jobs. If it all went away, right now, I'd be like, "All right. I don't really care."'
– Robert Pattinson

In the period between *Twilight*'s arrival in cinemas and the start of production on its sequel, Robert had been frank in interviews regarding the blessed-and-cursed situation he now found himself in, even questioning whether he wanted to remain an actor long-term. 'I'm not massively concerned about doing lots of acting jobs,' he confessed. 'If it all went away, right now, I'd be like, "All right. I don't really care." That's probably a stupid thing to say, but I don't, really. I think it'd be much worse to do a load of stuff that's really bad. Because then you can't go into another career. If you've made an idiot of yourself, you're never going to be taken seriously, as a lawyer or something, if you're, like, a joke actor. The only thing I want from anything is not to be embarrassed.'

Being interrogated by journalists for months on end had, he admitted, left him a little weary, not least because he felt he had nothing new to say and had been reduced to recycling the same answers over and over. 'I try and limit it [interviews] as much as possible. I don't really have much to say about anything. I've used up all my anecdotes and just start stealing other people's. I just watch other people's interviews and say what they say. But, I mean, it is a bit worrying, [that people might think] "That guy's like a tape, he doesn't even have a personality."'

Ultimately, it made no difference to Robert if he was asked about his acting or his hair – though he confessed his hope that he'd be remembered for more than his disorderly

Robert works the red carpet at Vanity Fair's *famously exclusive Oscars Party, after presenting at the Eighty-First Annual Academy Awards in Los Angeles, 22 February 2009.*

locks, which people continued to bring up even after he'd had them cut off. 'The only way to develop any kind of mystique is to completely shut up and never talk to anyone,' he pointed out. 'And I'm contractually obligated not to shut up.'

On 21 March 2009, *Twilight* was released on DVD. It sold three million copies in one day and remained at the top of the bestseller charts in several countries for many weeks afterwards. Robert reported: 'I was in a Blockbuster on the day it was being released. I had forgotten it was being released that day. There were two families who had come with eight- or nine-year-old daughters to get their DVD. They were standing in the line crying

> '**I don't want to be an actor for the sake of it. I don't find any particular pleasure in being an attention-seeker.'**
> **– Robert Pattinson**

and I stood watching what all this commotion was about. They didn't know I was stood there or anything. I was just thinking, "Wow, you're crying about a DVD." It's fascinating.' As the year went on, Robert's experiences of fan worship were to take on evermore extreme – and sometimes decidedly unnerving – forms.

Before the *New Moon* shoot began, Robert had told one writer: 'I don't know how they're going to make a movie out of it, because *Twilight*'s a love story, and *New Moon* is just – Bella's manic-depressive throughout the entire book. There's very, very little happiness, and there's nothing teen-y about it.' He saw his part in the second film as a

Three of hearts: Abandoned by Edward, a distraught Bella (Kristen Stewart) turns to Jacob (Taylor Lautner) for comfort in this promotional still from New Moon.

'supporting role', and, where in the book Edward features largely as a voice in Bella's head, in the movie the absent vampire would spend much of his screen time appearing to her as a ghostly hallucination, which meant Robert undertaking a lot of green-screen work with director Chris Weitz and the special effects team, who, he explained, 'designed a thing that basically allowed me to stand on a green box and stay relatively expressionless, and all these machines did the acting for me. Just the way I like it.'

'It is interesting,' offered screenwriter Melissa Rosenberg. 'He [Edward] isn't physically in *New Moon* a lot, but he is very much a presence throughout the book. That was the challenge of the script, how to keep him alive in the same way the book does and stay true to the book. I think we found a way to do that.'

> 'I think this is a darker movie.'
> – Robert Pattinson

Newly recruited director Weitz was by all accounts an instant hit with the cast and crew; everyone from Robert and Kristen to Stephenie Meyer praised the calm and efficient manner in which he ran the set and created an easygoing working environment for everyone involved. 'It's such a different film,' Robert said. 'I mean Catherine [Hardwicke] has a purity about her and a kind of completely uncynical viewpoint about the world. And I think Chris is a little bit more cynical and sort of looks at things in a little bit of a darker way. I think this is a darker movie.'

In-the-know fans hoping for a glimpse of their idols frequently besieged the film's sets, and

Robert (in full Edward Cullen make-up) and Kristen laugh between takes on New Moon's *Vancouver set, April 2009.*

> '*Twilight* made so much money that now you get judged not by how good the film is but how much money the film you're in is making. That's the scary thing now.'
> – Robert Pattinson

were sometimes obliged by cast members with autographs and photo opportunities, though the security surrounding what was now recognised as a full-blown pop culture phenomenon remained very tight. Robert himself sought to play this fact down. 'We had tons and tons of security,' he said, 'but at the end of the day, no one really knew where we were shooting. So it was kind of unnecessary. I'm walking around with three guys following me all the time, and no one ever turned up. There were never any *infiltrators*.'

Hotly anticipated additions to the *New Moon* cast included award-winning Welsh actor Michael Sheen, who would portray the sinister Volturi leader Aro, and former child star Dakota Fanning, who signed on to play the role of Jane, a cruel Volturi guard possessed of the ability to psychically inflict pain upon her enemies. 'I think Michael Sheen is amazing,' Robert enthused on set. 'I think it's really, really good casting for it. And I just looked at the big fight sequence at the end, and it's really, really cool... I just get beaten up – like, really badly.'

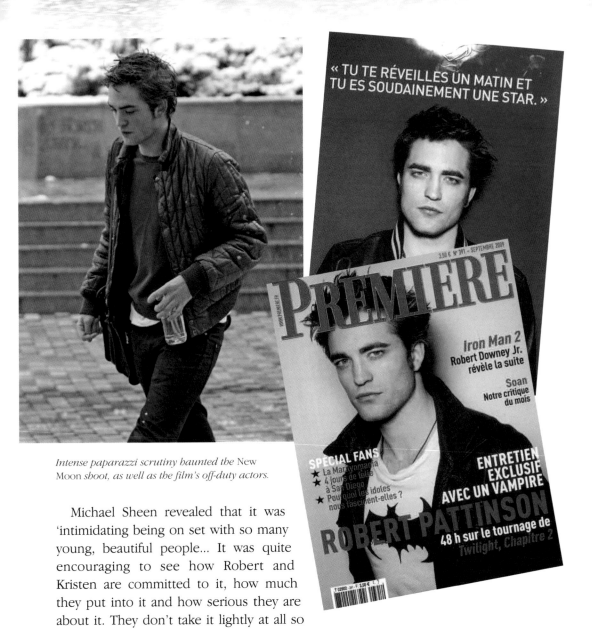

Intense paparazzi scrutiny haunted the New Moon *shoot, as well as the film's off-duty actors.*

Michael Sheen revealed that it was 'intimidating being on set with so many young, beautiful people... It was quite encouraging to see how Robert and Kristen are committed to it, how much they put into it and how serious they are about it. They don't take it lightly at all so that was great to see.'

Asked if the anticipation surrounding the film was making him anxious, Robert replied, 'A little bit, yes. I'm trying to fit stuff in between films. But it's nice at the same time to actually be doing something which people care about, because then you can put effort into something. And if people judge it badly, at least they'll be judging. At least they care about the outcome and they'll kind of analyse it or whatever. So you put enough work in, hopefully it will pay off.' The major anxiety that surrounded future films in *The Twilight Saga* was, Robert stressed, that the first movie 'made so much money that now you get judged not by how good the film is but how much money the film you're in is making. That's the scary thing now.'

The pressure created by the first film's success aside, Robert found shooting *New Moon* to be a more relaxed experience than *Twilight*, largely because that same success had given the filmmakers – and himself – confidence in his abilities. 'I was really beating myself up about stuff on the last one, but because of its success, I feel like I kind of know that a couple of things I did were okay. I have some kind of foundation, which I know will at least please an audience... maybe.'

During the months of the shoot, Robert and his co-stars were regularly spotted partaking of Vancouver's nightlife, and would inevitably find themselves the focus of public attention. Robert and Kristen were often seen sharing cigarettes outside the Blue Water Café and Raw Bar in the early hours of the morning, and Ashley Greene (who plays Alice Cullen in the films) had fond memories of a street called Robson, where the *New Moon* cast would jam with local musicians. 'I'm going to take up guitar,' Greene claimed, 'because Jackson [Rathbone], Nikki [Reed], Kristen and Rob all play guitar and sing.' Despite the global media focus upon the Vancouver set, and the gossip-magazine stories alleging an increasingly fraught on-set romance between Pattinson and Stewart, Robert maintained that the actors remained relatively unaware of the intense level of scrutiny they were constantly being placed under. 'It is strange. I was having dinner the other day and there was some magazine cover we [he and Kristen] saw. The movie is so insulated; someone was saying it's like being in the eye of the storm, but when you're in it, you can't really see what's going on. It seems like complete calmness. Then you look at magazine covers, and you realise it's actually a real magazine cover with us on and rumours that we're together. It sounds stupid, but people seem to believe it.'

> 'The movie is so insulated; someone was saying it's like being in the eye of the storm, but when you're in it, you can't really see what's going on.'
> – Robert Pattinson

Robert, in spite of his proclamations regarding the production's insulation from the wider world, was unable to leave his hotel without donning some form of disguise in the hope of avoiding the fans who kept a near-constant vigil outside. 'But instead I'm just getting more and more conspicuous; I'm wearing two hoods, a hat and sunglasses, which kind of stands out in the middle of the night. So I'm learning to sprint.' He also claimed

Soon-to-be-separated lovers Bella and Edward get misty-eyed over each other in another New Moon *promotional shot.*

that every time he went out, he felt as though he was on the job, regardless of whether he was actually doing anything work-related. 'I'm always in work mode. Just in case someone comes up to you, you've got to have your game face on.'

He did, however, choose to remain in his 'windowless hotel room on the thirty-something floor' long-term, rather than rent an apartment. 'I've settled there now,' he said at the time. 'It would take about three weeks for me to gather all my belongings. I don't let the maids in. I don't even pull the duvet down now because I don't want to see what's underneath.'

During the filming of *New Moon*, *Little Ashes* finally received a limited cinematic release on 8 May. While some critics praised the picture – and Pattinson's performance in particular – the majority of reviews were less than positive, and the film eventually grossed less than half a million dollars at the US box office, an outcome which came as little surprise to Robert. 'In an ideal world, everyone would go around watching arthouse films about Dali and Lorca,' he mused. 'But a lot of people have no idea who Lorca even was.'

On 13 May Robert celebrated his twenty-third birthday at Vancouver's Glowbal Grill and Satay Bar with his parents, Richard and Clare, and Kristen, who was accompanied by her older brother Cameron. The group were later joined by other members of the *New Moon* cast. They talked over Kobe meat balls and satay skewers, drinking beer and red wine until 12:30am. A few days later, the *New Moon* family attended a Sage & the Dills concert at the Metropole (co-star Nikki Reed is close friends with lead singer Sage), and continued to party with the band late into the night back at Robert's hotel room, where

Robert answers audience questions while promoting New Moon *at Comic-Con International in San Diego, July 2009.*

he strummed a guitar while Jackson Rathbone played harmonica. 'It's a very, very different experience,' Robert said of the months he spent shooting the film. 'Last time we were just kind of... it was so easy to get the entire cast together. We'd all have dinner almost every day and be able to talk about it freely and stuff. Now it's quite difficult to even leave the hotel. And all these random little stories become someway, somehow newsworthy, so you have to be very secret about everything. Even if you just want to clarify something in the script or something. It's just very different... It's very strange when you're aware of being observed, I guess.'

> 'Now it's quite difficult to even leave the hotel. And all these random little stories become someway, somehow newsworthy, so you have to be very secret about everything.'
> – Robert Pattinson

Having finished his work on the Vancouver leg of the *New Moon* shoot and flown from Canada to France, Robert appeared at the Cannes Film Festival on 19 May, where the now-customary fan frenzy ensued and he was shepherded from place to place by a team of burly bodyguards. 'I was at the last Cannes Festival when it really hit me how my life has changed,' he later admitted. 'I was in a restaurant, just hanging out, and when I tried to walk out of there two hours later, there were five hundred people waiting at the door. It was total chaos. I literally had to be carried to the car. It's ridiculous when you stop and think about it.'

Beautiful and damned: Robert Pattinson immortalises Edward Cullen.

Robert poses during a photo call at the Cannes Film Festival, May 2009.

'If you start thinking negatively about it then you go crazy. A couple of months ago I was going a little bit nuts; getting a little bit paranoid. But I guess now, you just learn ways to deal with things.'
– Robert Pattinson

On 21 May he took part in an AIDS benefit auction in Cannes, where, after taking the stage with Sharon Stone, he sold a kiss to the highest bidder. A peck on the cheek from the man of the moment eventually fetched $28,000. When quizzed about how he was dealing with the scale of fame he'd achieved in the past year, he replied, 'I guess I've found a certain kind of acceptance. You can't just keep going, "What's going on? I don't get it!" That gets old after a while. It is still strange, though... You can't really complain about it. If you start thinking negatively about it then you go crazy. A couple of months ago I was going a little bit nuts; getting a little bit paranoid. But I guess now, you just learn ways to deal with things. Anything which is so profoundly different, when it's new, it's quite difficult to deal with, and understand, but I guess I'm coming to terms with it a little bit.'

His whirlwind tour of Europe continued in Italy, where the concluding five-day shoot of *New Moon* took place in the picturesque medieval town of Montepulciano, located in the hills of southern Tuscany. Here, the pivotal scenes in which Bella rescues Edward from his fate at the hands of vampire coven the Volturi were filmed. Director Chris Weitz described the Italian leg of the shoot as a 'tremendous challenge' because so many people knew when and where the crew were going to be filming. Indeed, paparazzi photos and fan-filmed footage of the set and actors flooded the internet almost immediately. 'Everywhere that the camera wasn't being pointed there were hundreds of fans there,' Weitz said, 'and it wasn't so much that we minded them being there – as a matter of fact people applauded after every take, which

Robert runs a hand through his much-discussed hair at the world premiere of Quentin Tarantino's Inglourious Basterds, *Cannes, May 2009.*

Team Edward and Team Jacob go head to head.

> ‘I know a version of him better than anybody else in the world
> because I did this movie with him.’
> – Kristen Stewart

is unheard of. It was like doing theatre or something. But actually it was just the sheer logistics of getting through all the fans to get to the camera.’

New Moon’s producer, Wyck Godfrey, admitted that the furore surrounding Pattinson in Italy was particularly intense. ‘We tried to keep him from getting torn limb from limb,’ he laughed, perhaps only half-joking. Robert, for his part, found the sun-kissed Tuscan surroundings to be a source of fresh inspiration after three months in overcast and rain-sodden Vancouver. ‘The set [in Montepulciano], as well, the first sight of that. It just looked so bizarrely, eerily similar to how I’d pictured it from the book and the script. That was kind of astonishing. It was a good moment.’

‘Italy was intense,’ Ashley Greene confessed. ‘We literally all had two bodyguards and drivers, and we couldn’t walk and had to be driven around the set. It was because there were thousands of girls that came in from everywhere in the world to see [Robert]... They would sleep over and stay the night outside our hotel gate. It was nuts.’

No sooner had filming wrapped than Robert and the rest of his *New Moon* cast-mates reconvened in Los Angeles to attend the MTV Movie Awards on 31 May, where *Twilight* collected an impressive five popcorn-shaped gold statuettes: Best Fight (Cam Gigandet and Robert), Best Kiss (Robert and Kristen), Breakthrough Female Performance (Kristen),

Robert and Kristen shoot a climactic scene for New Moon *in the picturesque Italian hillside town of Montepulciano, May 2009.*

Breakthrough Male Performance (Robert), and Best Movie of the Year. When collecting their Best Kiss award, a playful Pattinson and Stewart teased the audience, leaning in to each other as if about to recreate their famous moment of lip-locking before Stewart broke off and exclaimed, 'Thank you *so* much.' Later, during her acceptance speech for Breakthrough Female Performance, a momentarily clumsy Stewart managed to drop and break her award onstage, providing another – albeit unintentional – moment of comic relief. In the past, Kristen had commented upon the inevitable closeness she felt with Robert after filming and promoting *Twilight*, which did little to quell the rumours of romance that dogged them, particularly when coupled with reports of Kristen's growing distance from her boyfriend of four years, actor Michael Angarano, and the fact that Summit – who undoubtedly relished the publicity such speculation provided – refused to publicly

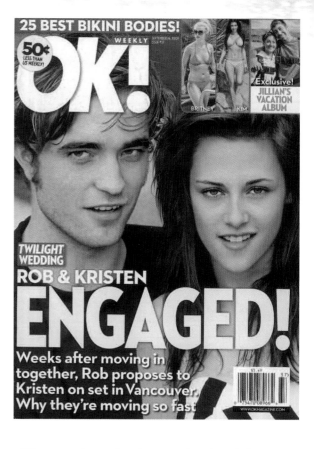

deny that Pattinson and Stewart were an item. 'We went through a lot together,' said the actress. 'It is crazy to go through something that heavy in real life. At the end of it you are inevitably going to have something. I know a version of him better than anybody else in the world because I did this movie with him.'

The MTV Movie Awards broadcast was also notable for featuring the premiere of the *New Moon* teaser trailer, which gave fans and the film's cast their first proper look at the forthcoming movie. On seeing it, Robert commented backstage: 'I was like, "Oh, okay. Taylor's been working out?"' – a joke alluding to co-star Taylor Lautner's muscular new physique, which he'd attained through a strict diet and exercise regime in order to win back the role of Edward Cullen's werewolf love rival Jacob Black.

> 'Now it's really out of control – out of your control. Your public image just seems to be in the hands of faceless strangers.'
> – Robert Pattinson

By June, the tabloid rumour mill surrounding Robert and Kristen's 'relationship' was in full swing, and issues of celebrity magazines like *Life & Style* and *OK! Weekly* were featuring Pattinson and Stewart on their covers on a weekly basis, accompanied by such unsubtle headlines as 'Yes, We're Dating. But Will It Ruin *Twilight*?' and 'Rob Tells Kristen: Make Up Your Mind!' Robert remained baffled by the abundance of what he insisted were elaborate

Robert and Kristen accept their award for Best Kiss – and tease the audience with the possibility of a repeat peformance – at the MTV Movie Awards, 31 May 2009.

falsifications. 'Now it's really out of control – out of your control. Your public image just seems to be in the hands of faceless strangers. You see these stories come up all the time and you're like, "Jesus. How do *you* know?"'

Despite his slight frustration at the press, he managed to maintain some perspective about the situation. 'I don't really care about it. I have the same little set of friends and I don't have anyone who would really get affected adversely [by inaccurate stories]. Every single person who they sort of romantically link me to... I just don't even really know anyone. So it doesn't really affect me that much.' This was a sentiment publicly shared by co-star Ashley Greene, who revealed: 'Rob's always like, "I don't belong here. What's going on?" He's not the most sociable. He's not one of those people who can go and talk to anyone. He's kind of a hermit and a little awkward. He got thrust into this limelight, but he's dealing with it. I think it'd be kind of difficult for anyone.'

'He's really talented, he's really smart, he's really musical,' said Nikki Reed, 'he's an intellectual, he reads. That's the side that I wish people would [ask about]. I don't know if anyone necessarily knows him... that side of him.'

When questioned directly regarding his and Stewart's supposed romantic involvement, Robert's answer was usually a weary, 'I don't even understand where that comes from,' or, 'Honestly, we are just friends.'

The fifteenth of that month also saw Robert begin filming *Remember Me* in New York City. A romantic drama co-written by Oscar-nominated screenwriter Jenny Lumet and co-starring Pierce Brosnan and *Lost* actress Emilie de Ravin, the film follows a young couple struggling to keep their relationship alive in the face of family tragedy. Robert explained that after being cast, he'd spent a weekend collaborating on the script with Jenny Lumet, and felt that Tyler, his character, possessed some of his own personality traits. 'She'd [Lumet] captured little bits of my voice and all the inflections and mannerisms I have.

> **'He's kind of a hermit and a little awkward. He got thrust into this limelight, but he's dealing with it. I think it'd be kind of difficult for anyone.'**
> **– Ashley Greene**

The character in the script is quite similar to me... There is a naturalism to the writing and I really felt a connection to it.' He went on to describe Lumet as 'incredible' and 'a genius', claiming that her script was the first one he'd read since before *Twilight* was filmed that he'd felt driven to pursue. 'I barely ever like scripts actually. After I did *Twilight* I really wanted to work but just didn't see a script I liked. I ended up doing nothing for a whole year. It was frustrating.'

Of *Remember Me*'s plot, Robert elaborated: 'I read somewhere that it was being described as the modern day *Love Story*. It isn't anything like *Love Story*. It is really hard to describe. It's about a twenty-three-year-old guy and knowing someone for six weeks. You don't just fall in love and say, "I'm in love," after six weeks. It's really a relationship story. It's very natural and the characters are incredibly real and well scripted. It's one of the few scripts I've read where you finished and realise you didn't really want it to end... I didn't go to acting school, I fell into it. I don't really have conventional taste, and I want to only do

A tired-looking Robert on the New York set of Remember Me, *where he was constantly besieged by overeager young fans, July 2009.*

Robert and his Remember Me *co-star Emilie de Ravin shoot a scene on location in New York, July 2009.*

'It's strange that you're doing a little indie movie, a very subtle story, and you've got like five thousand people watching you.'
– Robert Pattinson

films that I feel will be beneficial to my life. What we've moulded with *Remember Me* is a very exciting and subtle work. I don't really understand acting as acting. I'm definitely not one of those people who can just look scared when they're told to by a director.'

The eight-week *Remember Me* shoot, much of which took place on location at various locales around the city, was plagued by unprecedented levels of fan hysteria, and – despite the efforts of his security team – Robert was regularly accosted by grabbing, hugging, shrieking fans when being led between sets. Desperate cries of 'Please!' 'We love you *so much*!' and 'Oh my God! Oh my *God*! Oh *my God!*' trailed the actor wherever he went, and on at least one well-reported occasion, the situation became dangerous. After a morning spent filming inside the Strand Bookstore on Broadway and 12th Street, Pattinson ran into the road to avoid the screaming crowd of young girls who were stood between him and his trailer. In doing so, he narrowly avoided being run over by an oncoming taxicab. The vehicle reportedly grazed his hip, prompting one of his minders to shout, 'You see what you did? You almost killed him!' Although not seriously hurt, he was shaken by the incident, and thereafter the filming of *Remember Me* appeared to be taking its toll, with on-set sources reporting that Pattinson was eager to leave New York, where fan attention was

Robert pauses between takes while filming on the streets of Manhattan.
'What we've moulded with Remember Me *is a very exciting and subtle work,' he revealed.*

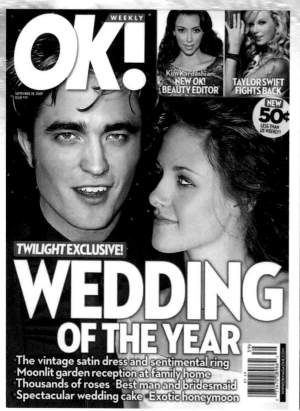

Left: Robert and Kristen discover the downside of life on the tabloid-fodder frontline. Right: *Taylor Lautner, Kristen Stewart and Robert Pattinson introduce the third and final* New Moon *trailer at the MTV Video Music Awards.*

more extreme and intrusive than he'd ever previously experienced. 'He's afraid that if he gives a hand, they'll take the whole arm. He's being advised by security not to encourage the crowd, so he doesn't even look up anymore.'

'Because of internet stuff and Twitter, there will be a crowd if you are in a place for more than half an hour,' Robert elaborated. 'I've learned never to stay in the same place for more than twenty minutes... The biggest challenge is coping with the crowds. I am a quiet, private person. It's strange. You have to change a little bit.'

'I've talked to Rob about it, and he's just paranoid all the time now,' said co-star Peter Facinelli. 'Like, even to go down to the Starbucks, he's ducking behind cars and does a roll-flip to the coffee shop. Then he gets up, and there's nobody there – but then the one time that he doesn't do that, that's when there's like ten thousand paparazzi jumping out of the bushes.'

Whatever he might have felt behind closed doors, Robert remained publicly unperturbed by the frenzy his presence was now capable of provoking in public. 'I can't claim anything to be a low,' he said. 'I pretty much live an almost identical life, apart from being recognised. That's not exactly the worst thing in the world... I had no idea people could get so obsessed. But it's not scary – it's amazing. People just project their idea of my character on to me and they just seem to assume I'm the same, when in reality I'm not.'

The issue of fans confusing fiction with reality had occasionally proven disturbing for the actor, as when he was confronted by a group of young women who'd embraced *Twilight*'s vampiric theme with more sincerity than was strictly healthy. 'One time there were these

Robert appears on the cover of AnOther Man'*s autumn 2009 issue (left), and in a May 2009* i-D *magazine spread.*

four girls, in Chicago, I think,' Robert recounted, 'and they had all scratched their necks until they bled and then when they came up to me they had these bleeding scabs. It was gross!'

Although he was changing hotels as much as once every two nights in an attempt to evade the more resourceful contingents of his fan base during the NYC shoot, he was able to find time to socialise in such hotspots as East Village watering hole Black and White (where he and Tom Sturridge drank on several occasions), Lower East Side restaurant Freemans, and renowned nightclub Webster Hall. At the Bowery Hotel he dined on quesadillas and beer in the VIP section, accompanied by Sturridge, Emilie de Ravin, his *New Moon* co-star Elizabeth Reaser (who plays Esme Cullen), and sultry actress Eva Mendes.

> 'Because of internet stuff and Twitter, there will be a crowd if you are in a place for more than half an hour. I've learned never to stay in the same place for more than twenty minutes.'
> – Robert Pattinson

'The most embarrassing thing,' Pattinson said, 'is when your friends want to meet up somewhere and you have to tell them: "Sorry, I can't come to that place," 'cause you know full well that the paps will be waiting for you there. I feel so narcissistic every time it happens, like the world has to revolve around me. I'm constantly looking over my shoulder; I need to stay ultra vigilant because, at any given moment, someone could be filming me or recording what I'm saying. It makes me want to work non-stop: at least on set, the level of security gives me some privacy. It's a relief.'

Eventually, the New York City Police Department went on record denouncing Pattinson's security team, and offered their services for his future visits to the city. 'His security people aren't up to the task of keeping him safe,' a source from within the department told journalists, 'and they have no idea how to deal with the crowds this guy attracts... This poor kid can't get in or out a car without things getting dangerous.'

'Rob cannot be in public and be static for more than five seconds without being mobbed,' exclaimed co-star Mike Welch (who plays Mike Newton in the *Twilight* films). 'If he's in a room and he looks down and he looks back up, everyone in the room will be staring at him. It's kind of ridiculous. [That level of fame] is literally Rob Pattinson and Barack Obama.'

'Where can the hype go?' Robert asked, before voicing his fear of fame's undeniable dark side. 'Unless I just get shot or something. That's what I'm afraid of.'

'I had no idea people could get so obsessed. But it's not scary – it's amazing.' – Robert Pattinson

On 23 July, with the *Remember Me* shoot nearing completion, Robert appeared at the Comic-Con comic book and arts convention in San Diego, sat on a panel alongside Kristen, Ashley Greene, Taylor Lautner, and Chris Weitz. The quintet embarked upon an in-depth discussion of the making of *New Moon* and previewed previously unseen footage of the film to near-constant screams of adulation from the audience. Jokes and tongue-in-cheek answers were in plentiful supply. When asked what he brought of himself to the character of Edward, Robert replied: 'I look a bit like him.' Chris Weitz, explaining his reasons for becoming involved with the sequel, said, 'I've been stalking Robert Pattinson for the last ten years, so when I had a chance to get within touching distance of him I jumped at the opportunity.' Quizzed on what she was looking forward to filming in the third and fourth *Twilight* movies, Kristen Stewart quipped, 'I can't wait to get pregnant,' which – beyond being a direct reference to Edward and Bella's baby in *Breaking Dawn* – was perhaps a sly nod to tabloid stories published in recent weeks which had alleged that Stewart was carrying Pattinson's child.

After Comic-Con, Robert and Kristen shared a limo during the three-hour drive from San Diego to Los Angeles, where Stewart was finishing work on Joan Jett biopic *The Runaways,* and Robert was spending a few days before flying back to New York to film his last scenes for *Remember Me.*

In late July, with only a few weeks left before the cast were due to reconvene in Vancouver to begin filming *Eclipse*, Summit revealed that it had recast the role of villainous vampire Victoria, who plays a pivotal part in the third film, with Rachelle Lefevre being replaced by *Spider-Man 3* and *Terminator Salvation* actress Bryce Dallas Howard – daughter of Oscar-winning director Ron Howard. While the decision was initially blamed on 'scheduling conflicts', Lefevre subsequently released a statement claiming that she was 'stunned' and 'hurt deeply' by the eleventh-hour announcement. 'I was happy with my contract with Summit and was fully prepared to continue to honour it,' the actress told *Access Hollywood*. 'Summit chose simply to recast the part.' Summit responded by releasing a second statement in which they claimed Lefevre had

Between fiction and reality: Rumours of offscreen romance dogged Pattinson and Stewart's onscreen coupling.

committed to filming an independent movie named *Barney's Version*, whose shoot overlapped with *Eclipse*'s rehearsals by ten days, without notifying the studio. They labelled her comments 'untrue' and remarked upon her 'lack of co-operative spirit'. The rest of the cast were forbidden from publicly commenting on Lefevre's departure, and the conflict between actress and studio was subsequently dealt with by lawyers. Catherine Hardwicke later revealed that Bryce Dallas Howard had been Summit's first choice for the role of Victoria when they were casting *Twilight*, but at the time Howard and her representatives had considered the part 'too small'.

On 9 August, the cast of the first film – minus Lefevre – attended the Teen Choice Awards in Los Angeles, where *Twilight* swept the board, scooping up eleven of the twelve awards it had been nominated for, including Best Actor and Choice Male Hottie for Robert. During his acceptance speeches Pattinson thanked the fans and described his involvement with the films as 'a very special experience'. Two days before the awards, Robert and Kristen had been photographed by an eagle-eyed *Twilight* fan leaving a Bobby Long concert together, where they reportedly watched Robert's old friend and musical collaborator perform from behind a curtained-off area of the venue – a sighting which further fuelled speculation that they were dating, particularly when Robert was spotted driving away from Kristen's house and Kristen was seen leaving the Chateau Marmont via a side entrance while Robert was in residence at the hotel. With the hype surrounding the franchise only set to gather momentum as *New Moon*'s release date approached, it seemed as if the intense scrutiny and speculation the pair had been subjected to in recent months would not be coming to an end any time soon. 'I can't remember what my normal life is like,' Robert admitted, perhaps not without a small trace of regret. 'A few months back, I came this close to breaking down; I was getting so paranoid. And then I started a new job and things started falling into place. I can't just turn my back on the situation and ignore it. If I said tomorrow, "Okay, I've had as much as I can take, it all ends now," it wouldn't change a thing. I may as well try to accept it and stay unfazed, since it's all completely out of my hands. I'm a fairly modest kind of guy, so it's not always easy. Though whinging about it will get me nowhere...'

'Every part is so different... I don't pick them in terms of genre; purely the script. If I like the script and I like the part, then that's all that matters.'
– Robert Pattinson

By mid-August, *The Twilight Saga* cast – finally completed by the addition of Robert and Kristen, who were the last to fly into the city – had once again reconvened in Vancouver, ready to begin filming *Eclipse*. The third instalment of the series would shoot from 17 August to 31 October, and following *New Moon*'s unveiling on 20 November, was scheduled to hit cinemas in July 2010. In May, Robert had confirmed that he was committed to *Breaking Dawn*, and estimated that all four films would have been filmed within an eighteen-month period. 'I think all of them will be done within a year and a half. The whole thing is about change and ageing. So it would look ridiculous if I'm playing seventeen when I look thirty-five.'

'I may as well try to accept it and stay unfazed,' said Robert of the furore that has risen up around him, 'since it's all completely out of my hands.'

'A few months back, I came this close to breaking down,' Robert admitted. 'I was getting so paranoid. And then I started a new job and things started falling into place.'

On 13 September, Robert, Kristen and Taylor Lautner temporarily abandoned the *Eclipse* shoot and flew to New York to attend MTV's Video Music Awards, where the trio of young actors collectively introduced the premiere of the third extended trailer for *New Moon*, which placed special-effects-laden emphasis on Edward and Bella's traumatic separation, and their climactic confrontation with the Volturi. The final countdown to the hugely anticipated film's arrival in cinemas had well and truly begun.

> **'It's just so frustrating when you read so many scripts and so many films are made every year that are simply designed to make money.'**
> **– Robert Pattinson**

Following completion of the third film in *The Twilight Saga*, Robert is due to remain busy, having committed to the role of Phineas in *Unbound Captives*. Written and directed by veteran actress Madeleine Stowe, the epic western co-stars Rachel Weisz and Hugh

Jackman, and focuses on the plight of a bereaved woman attempting to reclaim her children after they are kidnapped by a tribe of Indians. Shooting is scheduled to begin before the end of 2009, and will include location work in New Zealand and Mexico. Following that, Robert is committed to appear in *Bel Ami*, an adaptation of Guy de Maupassant's 1885 novel about corrupt 19th-century Parisian society, in which he will play Georges Duroy, a character he describes as 'totally immoral'. 'I judge things purely on the script,' he says of his non-*Twilight* film choices. 'I'm booked up for this year. I've been doing the most different things you can possibly imagine. Every part is so different... I don't pick them in terms of genre; purely the script. If I like the script and I like the part, then that's all that matters.'

The young star has also deflected suggestions that his role in the *Twilight* films will lead to him being permanently typecast. 'That's not something I'm afraid of,' he shrugged. 'Whenever I go to meetings for other projects, no one there seems worried by the blend of Edward Cullen and me. It's more like, "If you're interested in the role and you can bring *Twilight*'s audience to our film, then it's yours." They'd even let me play a woman, I think.'

'You can never be known for what you want to be known for. People will know you for whatever they want to know you for.'
– Robert Pattinson

Robert is well aware that his newfound status will provide him with the opportunity to make work that he cares about and believes in; to make a difference in an industry driven by commerce rather than creativity. 'It's just so frustrating when you read so many scripts and so many films are made every year that are simply designed to make money,' he acknowledged. 'It's purely business now. Out of show business there is no show anymore. It's just business and it's a template thing, and yet there are still a few people who are striving to just make something good and try to market it that away – as something good. If everyone did that, then this little problem in the film industry where virtually everything made is rubbish would end if everyone started trying to make good stuff instead of just trying to make money.'

Robert Pattinson's meteoric rise and phenomenal fame is of a kind bestowed upon an actor once a generation, but the question of whether he will ever be able to escape the shadow of the franchise that has provided him with global recognition does not yet have an answer. Whatever opportunities he pursues or decisions he makes in the future, one fact remains – a fact that Robert himself has acknowledged. 'You can never be known for what you want to be known for,' he shrugs. 'People will know you for whatever they want to know you for.'

Robert attends the Teen Choice Awards in Universal City, shortly before returning to Vancouver to begin filming Eclipse, *the third film in* The Twilight Saga.

Copyright © 2009, 2010 by Plexus Publishing Limited
Published by Plexus Publishing Limited
25 Mallinson Road
London SW11 1BW
www.plexusbooks.com

British Library Cataloguing in Publication Data

Stenning, Paul.
    The Robert Pattinson album. - 2nd ed.
    1. Pattinson, Rob. 2. Motion picture actors and actresses -
    Great Britain - Biography.
    I. Title
    791.4'3'028'092-dc22

    ISBN-13: 978-0-85965-452-4
    ISBN-10: 0-85965-452-4

Cover and book design by Coco Wake-Porter
Front cover photograph by Stephane Cardinale/ People Avenue/
Corbis; Kevin Mazur/ Wireimage/ Getty Images;
back cover photograph by Vittorio Zunino Celotto/ Getty Images
Printed by Scotprint

Acknowledgements
A book such as this cannot be completed – especially on time –
without the help, patience and perseverance of a lot of people. Special
thanks to our editorial team: Tom Branton who stepped in with his
meticulous attention to detail, additional writing and editing, Alisande
Orme for her speedy and sterling additional research, endless
watching and transcribing of every video and YouTube interview with
Robert Pattinson. Coco Wake-Porter for her endless patience
researching the photographs and designing the book. Thanks also to
Harvey Weinig and Alice Morey for researching material from the
United States. We would especially like to thank Monica Weller, Tara
Ripke, Joy Scaglione, Isabel del Castillo, Luna, and all at Pattinson
Online, Kiki T.
    Robert Pattinson has given interviews to many newspapers and
magazines, and these have proved invaluable in chronicling his life
and career. The author and editors would like to give special thanks to
The Times, The Telegraph, The Daily Mail, The Evening Standard, The
Daily Mirror, The Sunday Telegraph, The Independent, The
Independent on Sunday, The Los Angeles Times, The New York Times,
Liverpool Daily Post, Birmingham Evening Post, Detroit Free Press,
The Boston Herald, The Irish Independent, The Scotsman, The
Glasgow Herald, The Austin Chronicle, The Irish Times, The
Sacramento Bee, The Globe and Mail, The Daily Star. Seventeen
Magazine, Girlfriends Magazine, Wonderland Magazine, Film
Review Magazine, Live Magazine, Rolling Stone Magazine, Tiger Beat
Magazine, Screen International Magazine, Interview Magazine,
National Enquirer, Empire Magazine, People Magazine, Heat
Magazine, Variety, The Hollywood Reporter, Entertainment Weekly,
Us Magazine, Pop Star Magazine, Celebrity Year Book, Star
Magazine, V Man, Vanity Fair, Vanity Fair (Italia), Teen Vogue, The
Atlantic, Quizfest, J-14, Blast Magazine, Death Ray, The Sunday
Paper, Mirror Celebs, CosmoGirl, Bliss, Sugar. For television
interviews Sunrise Daily Australia, The Ellen Degeneres Show, This
Morning, Newsround, The Tonight Show with Jay Leno, MTV News,
Richard and Judy, The Tyra Banks Show, GMTV. The following books
were used in research: Twilight: Complete Illustrated Movie
Companion by Mark Cotta Vaz; Robert Pattinson: Eternally Yours by
Isabelle Adams, Twilight by Stephenie Meyer, New Moon by Stephenie
Meyer, Eclipse by Stephenie Meyer, Breaking Dawn by Stephenie
Meyer, and Diary Of A Genius by Salvador Dali.
    We would like to give special thanks to all the Robert Pattinson
web sites, works of devotion which were extremely helpful as
referenced sources: Pattinson Online (robert-pattinson.co.uk),
robertpattinson.org, robertpattinsononline.com,
rpattzdaily.livejournal.com, robertpattinsonmedia.co.uk, spunk-
ransom.com, spunk-ransom.net. Thanks also to the following web
sites: stepheniemeyer.com, twilightthemovie.com,
bellaandedward.com, twilighters.org, hisgoldeneyes.com, summit-
ent.com, kristenstewart.net, twilightthesoundtrack.com, twilight-
online.org, , osoarts.org.uk, wikipedia.org, gm.tv,
entertainmentwise.com, people.com, empireonline.com,
femalefirst.co.uk, fortunekiki.com, myspace.com/lizzypattinson,
fametastic.co.uk, models1.co.uk, seventeen.com, virginmedia.com,
eonline.com, mtv.com, mtv.co.uk, mtv.co.uk/channel/tmf, film.com,
thecinemasource.com,vanityfair.com, salon.com,
entertainmentwise.com, premiere.com, teenhollywood.com,
darkhorizons.com, etonline.com, usweekly.com, sky.com,
timesoftheinternet.com, youtube.com, canmag.com,
portraitmagazine.com, virgin.net, bbc.co.uk, rottentomatoes.com,
imdb.com, harrodian.com, thsboys.org.uk, tmz.com, the-leaky-
cauldron.org, movies.ie, thisislondon.co.uk, ew.com,
popstaronline.com, mymovies.net, myparkmag.co.uk, cnn.com,
about.com, howtobemovie.com, littleashes-themovie.com,
harrypotter.warnerbros.com, vanityfairmovie.com, goodprattle.com,
mak net al.com, rottentomatoes.com, slashfilm.com, fearnet.com,
Baltimore.metromix.com, theglobeandmail.com, my.cineplex.com,
buzzsugar.com, amazon.com, inquirer.net, people.com, themovie-
fanatic.com, extratv.warnerbros.com
    Thanks are also due to the film distributors: Focus Features,
Granada Film Productions, Channel 4 Television Corporation,
Columbia TriStar Film Distributors, IMAX, Warner Bros, Warner Home
Video, BBC Four, All3Media, Independent Television (ITV), Contender
Films, Summit Distribution, Regent Releasing.
We would like to thank the following for supplying photographs: Getty
Images/Pascal Le Segretain; Getty Images/Film Magic/Jason LaVeris;
Getty Images/Junko Kimura; Getty Images/Dave Hogan/ Stringer; Getty
Images/Dave Hogan/Stringer; Getty Images/Dave Hogan/Stringer; Getty
Images/Franco Origlia; Getty Images/Franco Origlia; Getty Images/Pascal
Le Segretain; Getty Images/WireImage/ Tim Whitby; Getty
Images/WireImage/Ferdaus Shamim; Getty Images/WireImage/Tim
Whitby; Getty Images/WireImage/Nathan Shanahan; Getty
Images/WireImage/Nathan Shanahan; Getty
Images/WireImage/Alexandra Wyman; Getty Images/ WireImage/ Jemal
Countess; Getty Images/WireImage/Elisabetta A.Villa; Getty
Images/WireImage/Vera Anderson; Getty Images/ WireImage/
Dominique Charriau; Rex Features/Marlon Curtis; ITV/Rex
Features/Bad Mother's Handbook; c.Regent/Everett/Rex Features/Little
Ashes; Twilight stills courtesy Twilight/Everett Collection/Rex Features;
Rex Features/Tonight Show/NBCU Photobank; Action Press/Rex
Features; PA Photos/AP/Richard Drew; PAPhotos/AP/Matt Sayles;
BigPictures.com/Simon Robling; BigPictures.com; Corbis/People
Avenue/Stephane Cardinale; Corbis/dpa/Hubert Boesl; Rex
Features/c.Everett Collection; Bigpicturesphoto.com;
Bigpicturesphoto.com; Rex Features/c.Everett Collection;
Corbis/Reuters/Mario Anzuoni; Rex Features/c.Everett Collection;
Getty Images/WireImage/John Shearer; Getty Images/FilmMagic/Jean
Baptiste Lacroix; Bigpicturesphoto.com; Rex Features/c.Everett
Collection; Getty Images/WireImage/Kevin Mazur; Rex
Features/Freddie Baez; Getty Images/FilmMagic/Justin Campbell; Getty
Images/WireImage/James Devaney; Getty Images/Christopher Polk;
Rex Features/c.Everett Collection; Rex Features/c.Everett Collection;
Corbis/Sygma/Murray Close; Rex Features/c.Everett Collection;
Corbis/Retna Ltd/Armando Gallo; Getty Images/WireImage/Kevin
Mazur; Tower House School photograph; Bliss Magazine;
Cosmopolitan; Sugar Magazine; Barnes Theatre Company for
photographs from their production Tess Of The D'Urbervilles;
RobertPattinsonOnline; Harry Potter/Warner Bros; Vanity Fair Focus
Features/GranadaFilm; Ring of the Nibelungs Tandem
Communication/Channel 4 TV; Haunted Airman/BBC 4; Little
Ashes/APT Films; How To Be/How To Be Films/Dragon Digital
Intermediate; Bad Mother's Handbook/Independent Television (ITV);
Evening Standard; Entertainment Weekly; lifeandstylemag.com;
Rolling Stone; okaymagazine.com; Vanity Fair; The Guardian Guide;
GQ; Premiere; OK!; AnOther Man; i-D
    Every effort has been made to acknowledge and trace copyright holders
and to contact original sources, and we apologise for any unintentional
errors which will be corrected in any future editions of this book.
    The author wishes to thank his wife Isla for her constant support
during the writing of this book.